W9-AGT-797

DOVER · THRIFT · EDITIONS

Troilus and Cressida

GEOFFREY CHAUCER

Rendered into Modern English Verse
by
GEORGE PHILIP KRAPP

DOVER PUBLICATIONS, INC.
Mineola, New York

DOVER THRIFT EDITIONS

GENERAL EDITOR: MARY CAROLYN WALDREP
EDITOR OF THIS VOLUME: THOMAS CRAWFORD

Bibliographical Note

This Dover edition, first published in 2006, is an unabridged republication of the edition published for the Limited Editions Club, London, 1939. Chaucer's original poem is thought to have been completed by 1385. The Note has been specially prepared for this edition.

International Standard Book Number: 0-486-44658-1

Manufactured in the United States of America
Dover Publications, Inc., 31 East 2nd Street, Mineola, N.Y. 11501

Note

CONSIDERED ONE of Chaucer's finest poems, second only to *The Canterbury Tales* in richness and depth, *Troilus and Cressida* (*Troilus and Criseyde* in Chaucer's original) is based on Boccaccio's poem, *Il filostrato*, which deals with the same subject matter. Written in the 1380s, Chaucer's tragic verse romance comprises 8,239 lines cast in "rhyme royal" stanza form, divided into five books. While following Boccaccio's general plot outline, which united various aspects of the tale of the Trojan warrior Troilus, Chaucer nevertheless added many details and a contemplative, philosophical tone. The result was a work of rich maturity, carefully considered, imbued with reflections derived from Boethius' *The Consolation of Philosophy*, and underpinned by a profound moral and religious sensibility. Chaucer's poem is thus entirely different in spirit than Boccaccio's shorter, sensual romance.

In the story as presented by Chaucer, Troilus, son of the Trojan king Priam, is one of the greatest warriors in the Trojan camp, the scourge and slayer of countless Greek soldiers. Like many strong men, however, he is no match for the charms of a beautiful woman. The lady in this case is Cressida, the lovely and demure widowed daughter of the priest Calchas. Urged on by Pandarus, her wily and experienced uncle, Cressida eventually succumbs to her suitor's passionate devotion and returns his love.

Following the consummation of their affair, however, Cressida is sent to her father, who has deserted to the Greek camp outside Troy. There she falls in love with, and is loved by, Diomede, a Greek warrior. Full of despair over her faithlessness, Troilus confronts the mighty Achilles in battle and is killed. As his soul ascends to heaven, Troilus is able to laugh at the woes of earthly existence, since he is on the point of achieving heavenly bliss. And in the final stanza, the author calls on young people to realize the folly of immersing themselves solely in worldly love and exhorts them to dedicate themselves to God.

Thought by many critics to be the first great English novel, the work is presented here in a modern English version that does not attempt to be a literal rendering of Chaucer's verse (probably impossible anyway), but tries to preserve the spirit and flavor of the original. This version employs the same seven-line stanza favored by Chaucer, and as a result, there are the same number of stanzas as in the original, and the same number of lines. Replete with rich, vivid touches of social detail, realistic dialogue, humor, and the author's tender and sympathetic approach to his characters, *Troilus and Cressida* opens a window onto the concerns of fourteenth-century courtly life. In this masterly verse translation, the reader will discover not only Chaucer's compassionate outlook on the combination of joy and sorrow that is the human lot, but the wise and humane regard of one of the greatest medieval poets toward the participants in the sorrowful drama he records.

Contents

INTRODUCTION

READERS OF this tale who may be interested in sources will look in vain for the story of Troilus and Cressida in Homer, Virgil or any other classic authority. Homer mentions Troilus but briefly, in allusion to his death. It was the early and unhappy end of this youth that stirred the interest of the ancients. This was probably the subject of a lost tragedy by Sophocles, and the few lines that Virgil devotes to Troilus are to be found in a description of the manner of his death. To the ancients Troilus appears to have figured as scarcely more than an engaging youth, one of the younger of the many sons of Priam, remarkable for his beauty and his valor, who was slain in his first flower by Achilles. A career cut short so early obviously provided little opportunity for the development of tales of heroic exploit and adventure, and, so far as is known from surviving records, the ancients never got beyond this single and pathetic incident of the death of Troilus as the result of his rash encounter with Achilles. Cressida cannot be connected with any character in classical tradition, except in mere name, and the whole story of the love of Troilus and Cressida is of much later origin, or at least of much later record.

It is not impossible, however, that the legend of Troilus began to grow very early, and that even in classical times Troilus stories of greater extent and detail than those now known were current. However this may be, we know that later writers continued to be interested in Troilus, and two late Latin historians must be mentioned in this connection. They are Dictys Cretensis, of the late fourth century, and Dares Phrygius, of the sixth century, both of whom wrote rather brief epitomes of the Trojan war in Latin prose. But neither Dares nor Dictys helped the story of Troilus along very far, and neither of them contains any hint of the love adventures of Troilus and Cressida.

The first writer to develop this theme was Benoit de Sainte Maure, in his *Roman de Troie,* a long narrative poem in French written about the middle of the twelfth century. A hundred years or so later, Benoit's story was reproduced in Latin prose by Guido delle Colonne in his *Historia Trojana,* and from these two works not only the story of Troilus and

Cressida, but a great part of the whole body of medieval information—
or supposed information—concerning the Trojan war was derived. On
the basis of Benoit and Guido, Boccaccio told the story of Troilus and
Cressida in his *Filostrato*. On the basis of Boccaccio's *Filostrato* mainly,
Chaucer told the story in his poem, and on the basis of Chaucer mainly,
Shakspeare made the story into a play in his *Troilus and Cressida*. These
in briefest outline are the stages of growth of this story, but the reader
who desires more detailed information will find it in abundance in Karl
Young's *Origin and Development of the Story of Troilus and Criseyde* (1908).

It may seem strange that Chaucer mentions explicitly neither Benoit,
Guido or Boccaccio, though beyond question Boccaccio was his main
source. But Chaucer was telling what purported to be an authentic
episode in the Trojan war, concerning which these writers, approxi-
mately contemporary with himself, could not be regarded as authorities
of high value. Very discreetly, therefore, he put the whole matter of source
beyond debate by a blanket citation of a mysterious Lollius, whom
nobody could question because nobody knew anything about him—
though nobody would acknowledge such ignorance.

Although Boccaccio's *Filostrato* provided Chaucer with the main ele-
ments of the plot of his *Troilus and Criseyde,* the latter is far from being a
translation of Boccaccio's poem. This can readily be seen by examining
William Rossetti's study of the two poems, in a publication of the
Chaucer Society, where those parts of Chaucer's English that are derived
from the Italian are placed in a column parallel to the corresponding
parts of the Italian text. The most notable expansion of Chaucer is the
character of Pandarus, and there are very many omissions, but line for
line and phrase for phrase, one will observe an infinite number of those
minor details of incident, tone and color which give a real life to narra-
tive, and which derive from Chaucer alone. The mingling of sentiment
and pathos in *Troilus and Criseyde* with somewhat Byronic, but never bit-
ter, wit and cynicism is entirely Chaucer's. *Troilus and Criseyde* is, as
Professor Ker well said, "the first great modern book in that kind where
the most characteristic modern triumphs of the literary art have been
won; in the kind to which belong the great books of Cervantes, of
Fielding, and of their later pupils." "It is a tragic novel," continues
Professor Ker, "and it is also strong enough to pass the scrutiny of that
Comic Muse who detects the impostures of inflated heroic and roman-
tic poetry."

These very just commendations are perhaps sufficient warning to the
modern reader against the assumption that because Chaucer lived and
wrote five and a half centuries ago, he was therefore a simple-minded
person. The adjective simple is the last that should be applied to
Chaucer. When Chaucer referred to Christian theology and heathen

deities in the same breath, when he mingled the notions of medieval chivalry with those of classical antiquity, he knew perfectly well what he was doing, and the juxtapositions were as amusing to him as they are to us. If any reader of this tale feels inclined to put the gods of antiquity and the saints of the calendar on very much the same level, he need not hesitate to find in Chaucer a kindred spirit.

The critics have ever been united in praising Chaucer's *Troilus and Criseyde* as the most perfect of his completed works. Comparison with *The Canterbury Tales* inevitably suggests itself, but the stories of *The Canterbury Tales* were left by Chaucer as fragments of a noble plan never carried out. *The Canterbury Tales* is, moreover, a collection of short stories, one may say, and as such not rightly to be compared with the sustained effort necessary to the conception and completion of a highly organized narrative like *Troilus and Criseyde*. This work has frequently been called the first great English novel, and the comparison with the modern novel is not unjustified. The limits of space do not permit assembling here any selections from the chorus in praise of *Troilus and Criseyde*, but the reader must be referred to the three volumes, *Five Hundred Years of Chaucer Criticism and Allusion, 1357–1900,* by Caroline F. E. Spurgeon, Professor of English in the University of London, a work not only of extraordinary industry, but also of great and varied interest.

The whole of *Troilus and Criseyde* has never before been presented to English readers in a modernized version. The story was extremely popular in the time of Shakspeare, and a number of other plays on this theme, besides Shakspeare's own, were written and acted in Elizabethan times. Shakspeare's play, by no means one of his best, was probably prepared to satisfy a popular demand. But these old plays were all adaptations of Chaucer's materials and are scarcely to be regarded as versions of his story. The first three books were re-told in English verse by Jonathan Sidnam, about 1630, "For the satisfaction of those Who either cannot, or will not take ye paines to vnderstand The Excellent Authors Farr more Exquisite and significant Expressions Though now growen obsolete, and out of vse."

But the most remarkable effort of this kind was the complete translation into Latin verse, made by Sir Francis Kynaston, the first two books of which were published in 1635. This work was received with loud acclaim, and it would appear that many readers in that day found Kynaston's Latin easier than Chaucer's English. But English was then frequently regarded as an unsafe and impermanent medium of expression. Sir Francis Kynaston obviously thought he was performing a pious duty when he translated *Troilus and Criseyde* into Latin, thus securing it from all possible chance of decay. In this, it will be remembered, he had the illustrious example of Sir Francis Bacon, Lord Verulam, who in his later years undertook to translate all of his English writings into Latin, "for these modern languages," he opined, "will at one time or other play the bank-rowtes with books." But Bacon's English writings have not been kept alive by his Latin translations of them, nor has Chaucer's *Troilus and Criseyde* required the embalming process of a Latin version to preserve it for posterity.

Of the later modernizations of *Troilus and Criseyde* I need mention only the poet Wordsworth's metrical version of part of Book Five. Doubtless there have been many other and later attempts made by lovers of Chaucer to give *Troilus and Criseyde* a modern English form, but these enthusiasts have all fallen by the wayside, and as they have left no record of their labors of love, of them I can tell no tale.

Since this version of *Troilus and Criseyde* now presented to the reader does not seek to give a literal and verbally exact rendering of Chaucer's language, a thing beyond the limits of human power in a metrical rendering which would be both readable and true to the spirit of the original, the question of the particular readings followed among the various surviving manuscripts of *Troilus and Criseyde* is not of great importance. The manuscripts agree, on the whole, with remarkable unanimity, but anyone interested will find all the variant readings recorded by Professor Robert Kilburn Root, in his scholarly and exhaustive edition of the text of *The Book of Troilus and Criseyde*. But if this version of the story of Troilus and Cressida does not correspond word for word with Chaucer's, it comes closer to corresponding with it line for line.

Chaucer's unit of composition was his favorite seven line stanza, and since the same unit of composition is employed here, and since nothing has been added or taken away, it follows that the number of stanzas in the two versions is exactly the same, and in consequence, the number of lines. It cannot be denied that there are several moments in the progress of the narrative when one would gladly omit passages of the text. One of these is the long argument in the Fourth Book on foreordination, pre-destination and free will. But this was a favorite topic in medieval times. Chaucer derived the materials of the argument from Boethius' *De Consolatione Philosophiae,* and certainly medieval readers would not be surprised to find Troilus pondering such subjects during his lonely vigil in the temple. He comes as near to a solution as anyone has done.

I may add, finally, that the story of *Troilus and Criseyde* did not end its career of development with Chaucer's telling of it. The central figure of Chaucer's story is obviously Troilus, and the poem ends with the death of Troilus. But what happens to Cressida? With fine humane and artistic restraint, Chaucer leaves Cressida when she has satisfied all the needs of his story. Whether she lived happily ever afterward or not, he does not say—though presumably she had no right to live happily. Chaucer does indeed pass sentence on Cressida, and no one can have any doubt as to his judgment on her actions, but when he has said what he has to say, he pursues her no further. He was her judge, but certainly not her executioner.

This pleasant duty of avenging Troilus was performed by the Scottish poet Robert Henryson, "Sculemaister in Dunfermling," in his *Testament of Cresseid*. In this poem, Cressida receives such punishment as ought to satisfy the severest advocate of poetic justice. Abandoned by Diomede, she returns to her father's house, but she finds no rest there. Leprosy has fallen upon her, her beauty is gone, and her father sends her forth to live as other lepers live, by begging. There is one fine moment in the poem, when Troilus riding by with a company of his knights returning to Troy after a successful raid, sees Cressida standing by the roadside among other lepers, with her begging bowl in her hand. A flash of memory, but not of recognition, brightens in him for a moment, he throws a gift of money to her, and rides on his way without a word.

PROEM

PROEM

WHAT God, O Chaucer, thou wert wont to follow,
What God or Goddess seemed most high to thee,
Jove or Jehovah, Venus or Apollo,
For thou didst honor each in his degree
And praise each for his special faculty,
If I but knew, upon his shrine I'd lay
This little book, my grateful thanks to pay.

But since I do not know and cannot tell,
And doubt if you spent many sleepless hours
Upon this point, it may be just as well
To hasten lightly by the heavenly powers;
They have their heaven, so let the earth be ours.
To you alone this tale I consecrate,
Which here anew I've ventured to relate.

And if it seems to you a little strange,
That anyone such task should undertake,
And English into English thus exchange,
The same remark as you have made, I make—
Men speak not now as in past days they spake;
But let me, Chaucer, argue not the need,
For liking only prompts me to this deed.

Nor learned doctors have I in my mind,
Who love you less than they love commentaries,
Unless, indeed, some doctor I may find,
Who will forget his Dictys and his Dares,
And all his lore of schools and seminaries,
And take you without question to his heart,
One half yourself, the other half your art.

Forgive me, Chaucer, if I here shall say,
I do not find you full of mysteries.

The world is much the same from day to day,
And well you saw its incongruities,
Yet held things ever in their right degrees.
To God and Devil you gave each his due,
And of all wisdoms, this you held most true,

That nothing in the world is black or white,
Except the inner will that makes it so;
But will, we know, hath limits to its might,
And fates through circumstances often grow.
All this in Cressida you well do show,
Reminding us, when she from Troy departs,
That pity still abides in gentle hearts.

And now what shall I say of Troilus,
Betrayed by life at his first entry there?
A noble mind, however generous,
Alas, an evil fortune may ensnare.
'Tis sad, but true, that virtue cannot share
Its qualities with any other mind;
It thrives within, and outwardly is blind.

But now enough of such abstract reflections!
The tale is worth a million such as these,
With its rejoicings and its sad dejections,
For both sides of the double story please;
For man is glad, when he misfortune sees,
That no such sad disasters on him fall,
And joy of others echoes in us all.

So come and read, though with experienced eyes,
For tales of love are meant for middle age;
But if experience teaches otherwise,
Pray disregard this observation sage,
And like all youth, in love itself engage;
Yet time that dulls the edge of every grief,
From ardent joys must bring as sure reprief.

One further word, ere I my tale begin,
Which may some question and some doubt remove—
Where change appears, don't understand therein,
The slightest wish on my part to improve;

To follow his own tongue it doth behoove
Each man, and one must yield, from time to time,
To pressing exigencies of the rhyme.

Besides, a thing unguessed of in your day,
Your lines with time have really shorter grown,
For many syllables have worn away,
And I to take their place have sometimes thrown
Into the lines new phrases of my own,
Which add to meter, to meaning not a whit—
You knew this trick, and made good use of it.

To add nor take away have I designed,
But trust your plain intent my story shows,
And have, indeed, my words more close confined
To yours, than yours are to Boccaccio's,
Your author, whom as Lollius you chose
To call, a fancy name that you invoke,
I take it, as a harmless private joke.

One further echo of your former time
I fain would think my lines have rightly caught.
I mean the rhythmic music and the rhyme
Which came to you, not far and subtly sought,
But as the native shadow of your thought;
For in your lines the poet ever sings
The deep sincerity of simple things.

Too high a hope I hold not in my heart
That I have done all this successfully;
To bring the past to life again by art
Demands the magic of high poetry.
But if I have not that, then let me be
Content if I achieve this single end,
And make new friends for him I count my friend.

Then go, little book, and may thy readers see
Herein some freshness of an elder day;
But let them just as truly find in thee
Echoes of life beyond all changing play
Of time and clime; and let them with me pray,
That love and beauty, ever fresh and young,
May never pass unheeded and unsung!

"Bot for men sein, and soth it is,
That who that al of wisdom writ,
It dulleth ofte a mannes wit
To him that schal it al dai rede,
For thilke cause, if that ye rede,
I wolde go the middel weie
And wryte a bok betwen the tweie,
Somwhat of lust, somewhat of lore,
That of the lasse or of the more
Som man mai lyke of that I wryte."

GOWER, *Confessio Amantis*

BOOK I—
THE TEMPLE DOOR

THE TEMPLE DOOR

THE double sorrow of Troilus to tell,
Unhappy son of Priam, king of Troy,
And how he fared, when first in love he fell,
From woe to weal, then back again from joy,
Until we part my time I shall employ.
Tisiphone, now help me to endite
These woful lines, that weep e'en as I write!

On thee I call, Goddess malevolent,
Thou cruel Fury, grieving ever in pain!
Help me, who am the sorrowful instrument
That lovers use their sorrows to complain;
For truly this is not a saying vain,
A gloomy man should have a gloomy mate,
And faces sad, those who sad tales relate.

For I to serve Love's servants ever try,
Yet dare not seek, for my unlikeliness,
The aid of Love, although for love I die,
So far am I from prospect of success.
But yet if this may make the sorrows less
Of any lover, or may his cause avail,
The thanks be his and mine this toilsome tale.

But O ye lovers, bathed in bliss always,
If any drops of pity in you be,
Recall the griefs gone by of other days,
And think sometimes upon the adversity
Of other folk, forgetting not that ye
Have felt yourselves Love's power to displease,
Lest ye might win Love's prize with too great ease.

And pray for those who suffer in the plight
Of Troilus, as I shall tell you here,
Beseeching Love to bring them to delight;

And pray for me as well, to God so dear,
That I may have the skill to make appear,
In this unhappy tale of Troilus,
How dark may be love's ways and treacherous.

And pray for those that dwell in love's despair,
For which they never hope to be restored;
And pray for them who must the burden bear
Of slanderous tongue of lady or of lord;
Pray God that he the faithful may reward,
And to the hopeless grant a quick release
And bring them from unrest to lasting peace.

And pray for lovers all who are at ease,
That they may still continue to be so,
And pray that they their ladies still may please
And unto Love a reverent honor show;
For thus I trust my soul in truth shall grow,
Praying for those who Love's commands fulfill,
And setting forth their fates in all good will,

With pity and compassion in my heart,
As though I brother were to lovers all.
Now take, I pray, my story in good part;
Henceforth I shall endeavor to recall
What sorrows once on Troilus must fall
In loving Cressida, who first returned
His love, but for new love this old love spurned.

WELL known the story, how the Greeks so strong
In arms, went with a thousand vessels sailing
To Troy, and there the Trojan city long
Besieged, and after ten years' siege prevailing,
In divers ways, but with one wrath unfailing,
Avenged on Troy the wrong to Helen done
By Paris, when at last great Troy was won.

Now so it chanced that in the Trojan town,
There dwelt a lord of rank and high degree,
A priest named Calchas, of such great renown
And in all science such proficiency,
That he knew what the fate of Troy would be,
For at the shrine at Delphi he had heard
Phoebus Apollo's dire forboding word.

When Calchas found his priestly computation
Confirmed the oracle Apollo spake,
That with the Greeks came such a mighty nation,
That in the end the city they would take,
He straight resolved the Trojans to forsake;
For by his divinations well he knew
That Troy was doomed, for all that Troy might do.

With stealth to leave the city he prepared,
For cunning plans he knew well to devise;
In secret to the Grecian host he fared,
Where they received him in most courtly wise,
As one of high distinction in their eyes;
For they had hope that by his priestly skill,
He might ward off their future harm and ill.

Great cry arose when it was first made known
Through all the town, and everywhere was told,
That Calchas had turned traitor and had flown,
And to the Greeks his faithless honor sold;
And every Trojan, both the young and old,
Declared that Calchas, with his wicked kin,
Deserved to burn alive for this great sin.

NOW Calchas left behind him when he fled,
Innocent of this so false and wicked deed,
His daughter, who in grief her life now led,
For mortal fear she felt in her great need,
And had no one in Troy her cause to plead,
For she a widow was without a friend
Who might bear aid and helpful counsel lend.

Cressida was the name this lady bore,
And in the Trojan city, to my mind,
Was none so fair, for in her beauty more
Angelical she seemed than human kind,
As though a thing immortal were combined
Of all of heaven's gifts of choicest worth,
And sent down here in scorn of our poor earth.

This lady could in no way close her ears
To her own father's evil deed and fame,
And driven near distracted by her fears,
In widow's sober habit dressed, she came

Before great Hector, where she doth proclaim
Her loyalty with tearful voice and eye,
And pleads for grace and treason doth deny.

Now Hector was a man of kindly heart,
And when he saw how great was her distress,
And then her beauty likewise played a part,
These words of comfort to her did address:
"About your father's wicked deeds, the less
That's said the better! But you yourself in joy
Dwell here with us the while you will in Troy!

"And all respect that men owe unto you,
As though your father still were dwelling here,
That shall you have, and all regard that's due
Your person, I assure you without fear."
She humbly thanked him for these words of cheer,
And would have thanked him more had he desired,
And took her leave and to her home retired.

And there she dwelt with such a retinue
As fitting was for one of her high station,
And kept good house, as she was wont to do,
Enjoying love and honest reputation
As much as any in the Trojan nation;
But if she children had, I do not know,
I have not heard, and therefore let it go.

THE fates of war were there exemplified
Between the Trojan and the Grecian forces,
For one day those of Troy were sorely tried,
But next the Greeks, for all their great resources,
Must yield; for Fortune hath uncertain courses,
And now her wheel goes up, and now goes down,
And now she wears a smile and now a frown.

But how this town came to its final end
Is not my purpose at this time to tell,
For much too far that lengthy tale would bend
Me from my point, and weary you as well;
But all the Trojan deeds, as there they fell,
Do Homer, Dares and Dictys all narrate,
For future time to read and contemplate.

Now though the Greeks the Trojan city hold,
Emprisoned by a siege set all around,
The Trojans still observe their customs old,
Honoring their gods with worshipping profound;
And of their relics one the most renowned
Was called Palladion, to which they prayed
In trust of heaven's protection and of aid.

And so it chanced when April heralds Spring,
And clothes the meadows with new pleasant green,
And when fresh flowers, white and red, now bring
Once more their fragrances so pure and clean,
The throngs of Trojan folk might then be seen,
All going forth Palladion's feast to hold,
According to their rites and customs old.

And to the temple in their very best,
The common folk came in from left and right,
And to Palladion themselves addressed;
And there came also many a lusty knight,
Many a lady fair and maiden bright,
All well arrayed, from greatest unto least,
In honor of the season and the feast.

Among the folk was Cressida that day,
All clothed in black, in widow's proper wise,
Yet as the alphabet begins with A,
So stood her beauty peerless in men's eyes;
And all folk gazed at her in glad surprise,
To see in her how fair the fairest are,
And under inky cloud, so bright a star

As was fair Cressida, so brightly shone
Her beauty there beneath her widow's weeds,
And yet she stood apart and all alone,
Behind the throng, which she but little heeds,
And by the door through which the crowd proceeds,
Quite simply dressed, but with the sprightly air
Of one who of herself can take good care.

NOW Troilus, the leader of a band
Of youthful knights, went with them up and down
In this great temple, where on every hand

They eyed the beauties of the Trojan town;
For Troilus prized neither smile nor frown
Of one particular, and fancy free,
He praised or criticized impartially.

And as he roamed about, he kept an eye
On all the members of his retinue,
And if some knight or squire heaved a sigh,
Or longing glances towards some maiden threw,
Then he would smile and make a great ado,
And twit him thus, "God knows she sleepeth blithe,
For all of thee, though thou shalt twist and writhe!

"The fashion of you lovers I have heard,
And heard of all your foolish gaits and ways,
And what great toils to win love are incurred,
In keeping it, what dangers and dismays,
For when your prey is lost, come woful days!
What fools ye be, and in your folly blind,
Who can no lesson in each other find."

And with that word he lifteth up his brows,
As one should say, "Now is not this well spoken!"
And straight these vaunts the God of Love arouse
To wrath, of which he gives a dreadful token,
For now he shows his bow is far from broken,
And suddenly he hits him fair and full,
And all such peacocks' feathers he can pull.

O world so blind! O blind all man's contriving!
How often things fall out in ways contrary,
Through vain presumption and conceited striving!
The proud and humble both are caught unwary,
For Troilus, who now mounts up so airy,
Hath little thought of afterward descending;
But folly oft hath unexpected ending.

As Bayard, when he feels his oats, grows proud,
And dances and skips out of the travelled way,
Until the lash upon his flank cracks loud,
"Although I prance here first," he then doth say,
"A leader in the trace, and fat and gay,
Yet am I but a horse, and by the law
For horses made, I still must pull and draw."

So fared it with this rash and hardy knight,
Who was a king's son of most high degree,
For though he thought that nothing had the might
To curb the heart of such a one as he,
Yet with a look, no longer was he free,
And he who stood but now in pride above
All men, at once was subject most to Love.

AND now I bid you profit by this man,
Ye worthy folk, and wise and proud withal,
And scorn not Love, he who so lightly can
The freedom of rebellious hearts enthral;
For still the common fate on you must fall,
That love, at nature's very heart indwelling,
Shall bind all things by nature's might compelling.

That this is true hath oftentimes been proved,
For well you know, and in wise books may read,
That men of greatest worth have deepest loved,
And none so powerful in word or deed,
But he the greater power of love must heed,
For all his fame or high nobility;
Thus hath it been and ever shall it be!

And fitting is it that it should be so,
For wisest men have most with love been pleased,
And those that dwelt in sorrow and in woe,
By love have often been consoled and eased,
And cruel wrath by love hath been appeased;
For love lends lustre to an honorable name,
And saves mankind from wickedness and shame.

And since you may not justly love deny,
Then take it as a virtue of the mind,
Delay not long with loving to comply,
For love at last must all constrain and bind;
And better the rod that bends, by force inclined,
Than one that breaks; and therefore pray take heed
To follow love, that best can guide and lead.

But now to leave attendant thoughts withal,
And come to Priam's son, of whom I told,
And passing by all things collateral,
My proper tale hereafter I shall hold,

Both of his joy and of his cares so cold,
And all the business of this sad affair,
As I began, I shall to you declare.

WITHIN the fane this knight his wit displayed,
Wandering at will and scattering jokes about,
And idly here, now there, his gazing strayed
On ladies of the town and from without;
And thus his roving eye, by chance no doubt,
Passed o'er the crowd and reached the very spot
Where Cressida stood, and then no further got.

And suddenly amazement came unbidden,
As more intent he bent on her his eyes.
"O Jupiter," he thought, "where has she hidden,
Whose beauty, shining bright, revealed now lies?"
And then his heart began to swell and rise,
But sighing soft that not a soul could hear,
He straight again began to laugh and jeer.

Among the small, this lady seemed not small,
She had a figure of proportioned kind,
Yet not the slightest mannish or too tall,
For nature had her frame so well designed,
And all her motions showed so well her mind,
That men could tell, in such there would reside
Honor and dignity and woman's pride.

And Troilus, the more he saw, the more
Was pleased with all her form and features clear,
But still she kept her eyes upon the floor,
Except she let one scornful glance appear,
As much as "Well, why shouldn't I stand here?"
But soon her eyes again grew soft and bright,
Which seemed to Troilus a goodly sight.

From eyes to heart in Troilus there passed
So great a longing, through this vision bred,
That in his deepest soul, fixed firm and fast,
This lady's image love did now imbed;
And he who once had held so high his head,
Must now draw in his horns and hold him low,
As one who knows not where to turn or go.

Lo, he who ne'er before had known defeat,
And scorned all who in Love's dominion lie,
He little was aware that love its seat
Hath in the glance and beaming of the eye;
Yet suddenly he felt within him die
All haughtiness of heart, by looking hurt,
And bless'd be love, which can men thus convert!

Thus still he stood, where he could well behold
This one in black, who hath his heart enchained,
Yet made no sign, and never a man he told
Why thus in that one station he remained,
But cunningly his purpose he maintained,
And now and then his gaze elsewhere extended,
Then back again, until the service ended.

And afterward, not dead but deadly smitten,
Out of the temple quietly he went,
Regretting all his jests and jibes hard bitten
At those in love, and fearing the descent
Of scorn upon himself, should he repent;
But lest this change of heart his friends might know,
With fine pretence he covered up his woe.

When from the temple all the folk depart,
Home to the palace he doth take his way,
Shot to the center by Love's flying dart;
But lest his manner may his state bewray,
He cultivates a bearing light and gay,
And at Love's servants still doth jest and smile,
Driven at last to such deceit and guile.

"Good Lord," he says, "you lovers are well paid!
See how the cleverest one among you all,
Whose duty is most faithfully displayed,
Must bear the whips and scorns that on you fall!
You get your pay, if pay one can it call,
Not good for good, but scorn for duty done;
In faith, your order is a goodly one!

"How vain are all your worship and your rites,
What small return you get for prayer or plea!
Your creed demands attendance days and nights,

No other asks such assiduity.
From folly love indeed is never free;
If I should tell all love's absurdities,
You'd call them slanders and base calumnies.

"But lo, the things you lovers oft eschew,
Or what you do with very best intent,
Your lady will be sure to misconstrue,
And say she knows it was not kindly meant,
Whatever cause she has for discontent—
Or none; she always holds the whip in hand.
How lucky they who join your happy band!"

But nevertheless, when he found good occasion,
He held his peace, the best thing he could do!
For Love had clipped his wings, and no evasion
Could help his case. Yet many a tale untrue
He told his friends why he from them withdrew,
Or if they noted his abstracted airs,
He told them just to mind their own affairs.

When in his room at last he was alone,
He sat down at the foot-end of his bed,
And first began to sigh and then to moan,
And then, through waking visions in his head
By fancy and imagination bred,
He dreamed he saw her near the temple door,
In form and shape as she had been before.

And then he made a mirror of his mind,
In which he saw her features all complete,
And thought perhaps occasion he might find
For such a lady's favor to compete,
And maybe might with her approval meet,
Or win from her at least sufficient grace
To grant to him a humble servant's place.

And he surmised the effort were not vain,
That in her goodly service he might spend,
And love for such a one, he dared maintain,
If it were known, all persons would commend,
Especially those whose hopes on love depend—
This was at first his line of argument,
Unwarned by any sign or sad portent.

The art of love thus minded to pursue,
He thought he would begin first secretly,
And hide his new endeavor from all view,
That friend nor foe the least of it might see,
But leave him chance for his recovery,
Recalling, too, that love too widely known,
Yields bitter fruit, though sweetest seed be sown.

Yet more than this—he gave much careful thought
On what to speak and when he should hold in,
And plans for leading her to love he sought,
And thought a poem straight he would begin
Upon his love, as aid her love to win;
For now his highest hope was set and bent
On ways to love—too late now to repent!

The content of this song when it was sung,
As given by my author Lollius,
Except for variation in the tongue,
Was word for word the song of Troilus,
And every word he sang exactly thus,
As I shall say, and as you now may hear,
If you will grant me your attentive ear.

"IF LOVE is naught, O God, why feel I so?
If love is aught, what nature then hath he?
If love is good, whence cometh all my woe?
If love is bad, it seems then strange to me,
How every torment and adversity
That comes from love, itself with joy doth link,
For still I thirst the more, the more I drink.

"And if I burn but with my own desire,
Whence comes my lamentation and my plaint?
Why should I grieve, when I with grief conspire?
And why should I unweary be, yet faint?
O living death! O grief so sweet and quaint!
How can it come that love should in me grow
Except that I consent it shall be so?

"If I consent, with wrong I then complain!
Behold how to and fro I merely toss,
Within a boat upon the wayless main,
While vexing winds each other ever cross,

And leave me rudderless to stand at loss!
Alas, what sickness strange in me doth lie,
With chill of heat and heat of cold I die!"

THEN to the God of Love anon he spake
With plaintive voice, "Thou, Lord, who solely hast
Taken my heart, and rightly dost it take,
I thank thee, Lord, for all that now hath passed!
For now that I have found my love at last,
My homage to her shall I ne'er deny,
But as her man, I still shall live and die!

"In her esteem thou hold'st a lofty place,
And for thy power such is rightly thine,
And therefore, Lord, turn not from me thy face,
But be thou gracious to me and benign;
For now my royal rank I all resign
Into her hands, and humbly standing here,
Become her man, and she my lady dear!"

No favor to his royal rank Love showed,
For from this flame no rank can ever save,
Nor parted from his customary mode,
For all he was a knight so bold and brave,
But held him in distress as thrall and slave,
And burned him in so many ways and new,
That sixty times a day he changed his hue.

So much from day to day his quickening thought
Now dwelt on her, and love thereby increase,
That every usual task he set at naught,
Yet often strove to make his burning cease
By sight of her, in hope to find release
From this uneasy burden that he bore—
But ever the nearer, ever he loved the more!

For ever the nearer, the hotter is the fire—
And this of course you know as well as I—
But were he farther off or were he nigher,
The eye of the heart that in the breast doth lie,
By day or night, with courage low or high,
Was still on her, with whom, she was so fair,
Helen nor Polyxena could compare.

And of the day there passed no single hour,
But to himself a thousand times he said,
"Thou good and gracious one, whom with all power
I serve, some pity cast upon my head,
For with affliction I am nearly dead!
Dear heart, gone is my joy and gone my life,
Unless your pity end this mortal strife!"

All other thoughts from out his mind had fled—
The Greeks and all his warlike reputation;
Desire new no offspring in him bred,
But reasons leading to one consummation,
That she on him would show commiseration,
And as her man, let him through life endure—
O what a life, for death, O what a cure!

Not Hector's nor his other brothers' feats
Of arms, in many sharp attacks well proved,
Stirred him to such like charges or retreats;
Yet nevertheless, wherever peril moved,
There was he found, and as he fiercely loved,
So fiercely fought, such wondrous deeds achieving,
They seemed to men almost beyond believing.

But not for hatred of the Greeks he raged,
Nor yet to aid the rescue of the town,
But mightily in arms he battle waged
For this sole end, to cast opponents down
And win his lady's favor by renown;
And so his warlike valor shone so splendid,
That fear of death on all the Greeks descended.

And love that made him bold, made him to sleep
The less, and still his multiplying sorrow
Such hold upon his heart and soul doth keep,
It stood revealed with each returning morrow
Upon his face, and he was fain to borrow
The name of other ill, lest men might know
It was the fire of love that changed him so.

He said he had a fever, was not well,
Whatever shyness makes a man to say,
But to his lady not a word could tell,

Although perhaps she guessed it anyway;
The fact remained, he got but little pay
For all his service, since she gave no thought
To what he had or what he hadn't wrought.

And then there fell on him another woe
From which his troubled mind could not be freed,
The fear that she might love another so
That his poor suit she would in no wise heed;
But though the thought made him at heart to bleed,
Yet never a move, for all the world to win,
To make his sorrow known durst he begin.

But in his moments of relief from care,
Thus to himself he often would complain,
And say, "O fool, now art thou in the snare,
Who once did jest at love and all its pain!
Now art thou caught! Now go and gnaw thy chain!
Thou once wert wont that love to reprehend
From which thyself thou canst not now defend.

"What will now every lover say of thee,
If this be known, when thou art out of sight,
But laugh in scorn and say, 'Lo, there goes he
Who thought he dwelt alone on wisdom's height,
And held all lovers in such low despite!
But now, thank God, his place is in the dance
Of those whom Love delayeth to advance.'

"But O, thou woful Troilus, would God
(Since love thou must, by thy sad destiny)
That one who knows thy woe should hold the rod
O'er thee, although no pity in her be!
But cold in love thy lady is to thee,
As frost is cold beneath the winter moon;
Like snow in flame, so thou must perish soon!

"Would God I were arrived safe in the port
Of death, to which my sorrow will me lead!
That were for me the best and last resort,
Then were I of all fear and longing freed!
But if my hidden sorrow men should heed,
I shall be marked and mocked a great deal more
Than any fool for folly famed before!

"Now help, O God, and help, my lady sweet,
I am your prisoner caught and none so fast!
Have mercy now, and help me to defeat
This death! And I, until my days are past,
With more than life will love you to the last.
Now with some kindly glance my heart restore,
Although you never grant me favor more!"

THESE words, and more, within his room he spake,
And begged his lady, in his grief profound,
Some recognition of his love to make,
And wept salt tears in which he nearly drowned—
But all in vain, for not a single sound
She heard, not being present to do so,
Which made his griefs a thousandfold to grow.

Lamenting in his chamber thus alone,
A friend, whose name was Pandar, happened there,
And coming in by chance, he heard him groan,
And saw his friend in great distress and care.
"What ho, my friend!" he cried, "Why this despair?
What nasty trick does fortune on you serve?
Or have the naughty Greeks got on your nerve?

"Or is remorse of conscience cause of this,
And have you turned reluctant and devout,
Repenting all that you have done amiss,
For fear your guilt at last will find you out!
God curse the Greeks who lie in siege about
Our town, and turn our joy into distress
By driving jolly folk to holiness!"

He spoke these words, as I them to you say,
That Troilus to anger might be stirred,
And sorrow thus to anger giving way,
To deeds of courage once again be spurred;
For well he knew, and well all men have heard,
There was among the Trojans none more bold,
Or none whom men in higher honor hold.

"WHAT chance," said Troilus, "what accident,
Hath led thee here to see my wretched state,
Where I deserted and alone lament?
But for God's sake, don't linger here too late,

But get thee gone, for surely my sad fate
Will be a painful sight, since I must die!
Then go, and let me here untroubled lie.

"But if you think that I am sick from fear,
It is not so, and therefore scorn me naught.
There's something else that touches me more near
Than anything the Greeks as yet have wrought,
And brings on me this sad and mortal thought.
But though I may not now to thee confide it,
Please don't be vexed, 'tis best that I should hide it."

Then Pandar, yearning for this hapless youth,
Replied and said, "Alas, what can this be?
Good friend, if faithful love or constant truth
Now is or ever was twixt you and me,
Then do not treat me with such cruelty!
A confidential ear I'll gladly lend,
For don't forget that Pandar is your friend.

"And I will gladly share with you your pain,
If it turn out I can no comfort bring;
For 'tis a friend's right, please let me explain,
To share in woful as in joyful thing.
Through true or false report, I still shall cling
To you in faith forever firm and fast;
So tell your woe, for tell you must at last."

Troilus heaved a deep and mournful sigh,
And said to him, "Perhaps it may be best
If with your friendly wish I should comply,
And tear my secret from my aching breast,
Though well I know you can bring me no rest.
But lest thou think I have no trust in thee,
I'll tell thee, friend, just how it stands with me.

"Lo, Love, against which he who most defendeth
Himself, the more thereby his effort faileth,
This Love so far his rule o'er me extendeth,
That now my heart to death a straight course saileth!
Love-longing over me so deep prevaileth,
That here to die for Love were greater joy
Than be both King of Greece and King of Troy.

"In what I've said, methinks to you I've told
More than enough about my cause of woe.
But for the love of God, my care so cold,
Conceal it well! For what you only know,
If further spread, great harms might after grow.
Now go, and live in joy and happiness,
And let me die, abandoned to distress."

"TO HIDE this from me was unkindly done,"
Pandar replied, "and it was most unwise,
For maybe you have set your heart on one
Of whom I might with profit you advise."
"Maybe indeed," cried he in great surprise,
"In love you never had the slightest chance,
How can you then another's love advance?"

"Now listen, Troilus," replied his friend,
"Perhaps I am a fool, yet it is so,
That folly oft can helpful counsel lend,
Whereby the wise the better way may know.
For I myself have seen a blind man go,
Where he would fall who sees both far and wide;
Sometimes a fool can be the safest guide.

"A whetstone is no carving instrument,
And yet it maketh sharp the carving tool;
And if you see my efforts wrongly spent,
Eschew that course and learn out of my school;
For thus the wise may profit by the fool,
And edge his wit, and grow more keen and wary,
For wisdom shines opposed to its contrary.

"For how might sweetness ever have been known
To him who never tasted bitterness?
Felicity exists for those alone
Who first have suffered sorrow and distress;
Thus white by black, honor by shame's excess,
More brightly shines by what the other seems,
As all men see and as the wise man deems.

"By opposites does one in wisdom grow,
And though I have in love vain effort made,
Then all the better I thereby should know

To guide thee on thy path when thou hast strayed.
Spurn not with scorn, therefore, my proffered aid,
For I desire nothing but to share
Thy grief, and make it easier to bear.

"Indeed I am a quite good parallel
To what Oenone once, a shepherdess,
To your own brother Paris said so well,
Writing in grief of heart and heaviness;
You've seen the letter that she wrote, I guess?"
"No, that I haven't," answered Troilus.
"Then listen," Pandar said, "for it goes thus."

'Excelling in the art of medicine,
Phoebus could rightly find for each disease
A cure, through herbs that he was well versed in;
But to himself his skill could bring no ease,
When love on him did violently seize
For old Admetus' daughter, king of Greece,
Nor all his art could bid his sorrows cease.'

"So goes it now, unhappily, with me.
I love in vain, that's why my heart is sore,
And yet it may be I can counsel thee
And not myself. Reprove me now no more;
I have no cause, I know, on high to soar,
As doth a hawk, when he would sport and play,
But still, that doesn't mean I've naught to say.

"And one thing you may count a certainty,
I'd rather die in great and mortal pain,
Than breathe a word of what you say to me;
You need not fear that I would you restrain,
Though it were Helen's love you sought to gain,
Your brother's wife; whatever be her name,
For me I'll let you love her all the same.

"In my good friendship you can rest secure,
If to me you will only plainly mention
The source of all the grief that you endure;
For do not think I have the least intention
To speak to you by way of reprehension
In this affair; for no one can prevent
A man from loving, ere his love is spent.

"That both of these are vices is well seen—
To trust all men or all men disbelieve;
But no vice enters in the golden mean.
'Tis right the word of some men to receive,
And for this cause, it should not thee aggrieve
To take me fully in thy confidence,
For I mean only good and no offence.

"Solomon saith, 'Take heed who stands alone,
For if he falls, there's none to help him rise.'
But since thou hast a friend, to him make known
Thy grief, for we can better ways devise
To win thy love in more effective wise
Than lie and weep, like Niobe the queen,
Whose tears remain in marble to be seen.

"So now give o'er this lachrymose distress,
Of things that lighten grief now let us speak,
For thus thy time of sorrow may seem less.
Take not delight in woe thy woe to seek,
For fools alone sorrow with sorrow eke,
Who when they fall in some mishap and grief,
Neglect to look elsewhere for their relief.

"Men say that 'Misery loves company,'
And this is by no means a saying vain,
But one in which we both ought to agree,
For both of us with right on love complain.
I am so full of sorrow, I maintain
Another single drop could find no place
To sit on me, because there is no space.

"I take it thou art not afraid of me,
Lest of thy lady I should thee beguile.
You know yourself I am not fancy free,
But serve a lady dear for this long while;
And since you need fear neither trick nor wile,
And if your trust and confidence I hold,
Tell me as much as I to you have told."

TROILUS answered not a single word,
And still as death he lay, though could but hear,
Yet afterward he sighed, and then he stirred,
Which showed that he had lent attentive ear,

And then cast up his eyes, so that great fear
Had Pandar, lest in sudden frenzy falling,
His soul might flit away beyond recalling.

"Wake up," he cried, with voice both loud and sharp,
"Hast thou in sleep by lethargy been struck?
Or art thou like the ass that hears a harp,
And hears the sound, when men the harp-strings pluck,
But from that sound no melody can suck
His heart to gladden in the very least,
Because he is a dull and brutish beast?"

Pandar from further speech with that refrained,
But not a word would Troilus reply,
For never once the thought he entertained
To tell for whom he thus must weep and sigh;
For it is said, "Man makes the stick whereby
The maker himself is beaten in his turn";
This bit of wisdom from the wise we learn.

And specially he planned few confidences
In love, for love should grow in secrecy,
Since of itself love breaks through all defences,
If one should fail to guard it zealously.
And sometimes it is art to seem to flee
The thing which in effect one is pursuing;
Such thoughts was Troilus in mind reviewing,

When thus so loudly he heard Pandar cry
"Wake up!"; then he began to sigh full sore,
And said, "Good friend, although so still I lie,
I am not deaf! Now peace, and say no more,
For I have heard your wisdom and your lore.
Leave me in peace my mishap to bewail,
For all your proverbs may me naught avail.

"You cannot find a remedy for me;
Besides I want no cure. I want to die!
And what care I for your queen Niobe?
You've told enough of old wives' tales, say I."
"Well, then," said Pandar, "let me but reply,
That fools alone their woes and griefs enjoy
And shun the remedies they might employ.

"It seems to me you must have lost your reason!
But tell me this, if I her name but knew,
In all good faith and with no taint of treason,
Durst I then tell her in her ear for you,
What you yourself have not the nerve to do,
And beg of her some little sign to show?"
"No, no," cried Troilus, "I tell you no!"

"What," said Pandar, "not even if I tried
As though it were my own affair and need?"
"Most surely not," sad Troilus replied.
"But why?" "Because you never could succeed."
"How do you know?" "I know quite well indeed,"
Said Troilus, "when all is said and done,
She will by no such wretch as I be won."

"O well," said Pandar, "it may quite well be,
That without cause you are thus in despair.
For look, your lady is not dead, is she?
How can you tell beforehand how you'll fare?
Such evils are not oft beyond repair!
And why must you the worst always suppose,
Although the outcome you nor no one knows?

"I grant you well your grief is quite as sore
And sharp as that of Tityos in hell,
Whose heart continually the vultures tore,
According to the stories old books tell;
But still I can't permit you thus to dwell
Under the vain and baseless imputation
You've caught an ill for which there's no salvation.

"If you refuse to tell, just for faint heart,
And for your sloth and foolish wilfulness,
And will no slightest hint to me impart,
And why I should not help in your distress
You will not give a reason more or less,
But supine on your bed yourself you stretch—
I ask, what woman could love such a wretch?

"And how can she account then for your death,
If you thus die, and she knows nothing why,
Except for fear you breathed your final breath

Because the Greeks about our city lie?
What figure will you cut in the world's eye?
Then she and all will say in scornful tones,
'The wretch is dead, the devil have his bones.'

"You may here weep alone and pray and kneel,
But if the one you love of this knows naught,
How can she make return that you can feel—
Unknown, unkissed and lost, who is unsought!
Lo, many a man his love hath dearly bought,
And twenty years opined were not too much
To win the right his lady's lips to touch.

"But should he therefore fall in dark despair,
Or as a recreant himself demean,
Or slay himself, because his lady's fair?
No, no, let love be ever fresh and green,
Let each forever cherish his heart's queen,
And think it is love's guerdon but to serve,
A thousandfold more than he doth deserve."

TO THESE wise words then Troilus took heed,
And saw the state of mind that he was in,
And thought what Pandar said was true indeed,
That just to die would not his lady win,
But would be both unmanly and a sin,
And useless, too, in every jot and tittle,
Since of his woe she knew still less than little.

At this sad thought, he sighed both loud and long,
And said, "Alas, what's best for me to do?"
And Pandar answered him, "You can't go wrong
In telling me your story whole and true;
I give my word, within a day or two,
I'll bring you news, the best you ever got,
Or have me drawn and quartered on the spot."

"That's what you say," cried Troilus, "alas,
But saying so, that will not make it so!
For my affairs have come to such a pass
That I perceive that Fortune is my foe,
And all who up and down this wide world go,
Must take whatever Fortune shall decree,
For as she will, she plays with bound and free."

"So then," said Pandar, "Fortune is to blame
For your own feelings! Now at last I see!
But don't you know that Fortune is the same
To all alive, in varying degree?
But of one comfort you have certainty,
For as all joys on earth are short and brief,
So time will bring for sorrow its relief.

"Because if Fortune's wheel should cease to turn,
Then Fortune she at once no more would be;
And since in no fixed place she may sojourn,
It may chance, by mere mutability,
Such good luck she hath now in store for thee,
And such a boon to thee she soon will bring,
That for the joy of it, thy heart shall sing.

"And therefore do you know what I advise?
Look up! Don't keep your eyes upon the ground!
The sick must first unto the doctor's eyes
Reveal in what respect he is unsound.
To Cerberus in hell may I be bound,
If my own sister were thy cause of sorrow,
For all of me, she should be thine tomorrow.

"If I had something clear on which to go,
I'd surely find the remedy you need.
At least say this, your lady do I know?
For if I do, the fight is on indeed!"
Then Troilus at heart began to bleed,
For he was hit, and blushed with rosy shame;
"Aha!" cried Pandar, "now I smell the game!"

And then his victim he began to shake,
And said, "You thief, her name you've got to tell!"
Then hapless Troilus, with many a quake,
As though his soul were being led to hell,
Murmured, "Of all my woe the source and well
Is Cressida—and now you know her name!"
And with these words, he almost died for shame.

WHEN Pandar heard who was his lady love,
Then he was glad and said, "My friend so dear,
Now all goes well, for by great Jove above,
You're lucky in your choice. Be of good cheer!

Of fame, wisdom and virtue never fear
She hath enough, and also gentle ways;
Her beauty you know, and I need not to praise.

"She hath besides a free and open hand
With all she owns, is affable in speech,
And how to do things well doth understand,
Yet never doth in doing overreach,
But gracious are her manners all and each.
Such truth and honor in her heart abide,
A king's heart seems a poor thing there beside.

"Good reason now you have to be content,
For half the battle is already gained
When courage dull inaction doth prevent,
And peace of heart within has been attained;
For love with every good is deep ingrained
When it is set upon a worthy place,
It is no evil then, but heaven's grace.

"You have this reason to be glad besides,
That since your lady hath these virtues all,
Then pity, also, in her heart resides,
Among these other things in general.
But take thou heed, whatever may befall,
That thou dishonor not an honest name,
For virtue never lends itself to shame.

"However, let us not be too austere,
For thou hast set thy heart in right good place;
But truth to tell, I always had a fear
That Love to you would never show his face.
And know you why? Because such vile disgrace
You heaped on Love, and Love did'st even call
'Saint Idiot, the lord of lovers all.'

"How often did you crack a foolish jest,
And say, 'Love's servants truly I disown,
For all are fools and God's apes at the best,
And some will munch their dreary food alone,
Lying abed with many a sigh and moan!'
White fever, you said, attacks the burning lover,
And often prayed such never might recover;

"And some, you said, lie shivering with the cold,
And on them turned your mockery full oft,
And laughed at those who fancied stories told
Of sleepless nights when they were resting soft.
With boasts, you said, they held their heads aloft,
But for all that, must bend low at the last,
And many such like jests on love you passed.

"And you maintained that for the greater part,
All lovers loved but in a general way,
Because they thought it was the safer art
A dozen loves at one time to essay.
Now I might make such jests on you today,
But won't, because I'm quite convinced in mind
That you'll not be a lover of that kind.

"Now beat thy breast, and pray to God above,
'Thy mercy, Lord! For now I do repent
Of all I've said, and deeply now I love!'
Pray thus, that thus the God may now relent!"
"Ah, Lord," cried Troilus, "hear my lament,
Who pray to thee my jesting to forgive,
As I shall jest no more the while I live!"

"Well prayed," quoth Pandar. "Now it can be said
Thou hast the God of Love in all appeased,
And since thou many a bitter tear hast shed,
And spoken things therewith thy God is pleased,
I feel quite sure thou shalt in all be eased,
And she from whom arises all thy woe,
Through her thou shalt still further comfort know.

"For that same ground that bears the useless weed,
Bears also wholesome herbs, and quite as oft;
And where the rough and stinging nettles breed,
Waxes the rose, so sweet and smooth and soft;
And next the valley, lifts the hill aloft,
And after night, then comes the glad tomorrow,
And so is joy the after end of sorrow.

"But hold with nicely tempered hand thy bridle,
And think that all things have their proper tide,
Or else thy labor is but vain and idle;

He makes most speed who can his time abide,
Who planneth well before he doth decide;
Be strong and free, and if you persevere,
All will be well, as I have made it clear.

"A man divided in a dozen places
Is nowhere whole, philosophy doth show,
For his own labor he himself effaces.
Do you know how this is? Why, just as though
You plant a tree or herb where it should grow,
And on the morrow pull it up alive—
No wonder if it thus should never thrive.

"And since the God of Love hath love bestowed
On thee full worthy of thy worthiness,
Stand fast, for to a good port hast thou rowed.
Let not thy hope and courage e'er grow less,
For only some great lack or some excess,
Or overhaste, can make our labor vain,
Whereby our happy end we shall attain.

"And know you why I am so well inclined
In this affair with my dear niece to treat?
Because 'tis said, with truth, of all mankind,
That never one dwelt on this earthly seat
But he must feel in some degree the heat
Of love, or earthly or celestial,
For love is planted in us one and all.

"As for this lady we have now in mind,
By reason of her beauty and her youth,
Celestial love is not so well designed,
Although she could love in that way forsooth;
But now it seems to me, to tell the truth,
She ought to love some good and worthy knight,
If she would do what's suitable and right.

"Therefore I am and will be ready still
To help you in whatever way I can,
For what I do hereafter surely will
Give pleasure to you both; and all our plan
We can so closely hide that never a man
Shall be the wiser in the least degree,
And so in fact, we shall be glad all three.

"And now there comes to me a right good thought,
And that it's good I'm sure you will confess
When all my meaning you have fully caught.
I think that since Love hath, in due process,
Converted thee from all thy wickedness,
That thou shalt be a pillar and a post
In his support, and grieve his foes the most.

"To prove my point, recall how those great clerks
Who most have erred against a certain law,
And are converted from their wicked works
By God's good grace that doth them to him draw,
Are just the ones who hold God most in awe,
And grow into his most believing band,
For they know best all error to withstand."

TO ALL this preaching Troilus assented,
Accepting likewise Pandar's proferred aid;
Then waned the woes by which he'd been tormented,
But hotter waxed his love; and then he made
Reply, with joyful heart, but manner staid,
"Now, blessed Venus, let me never die,
Till all thy words, O Pandar, fructify!

"But friend, how shall my pain grow less acute
Till this is done? And also tell me first,
What thou wilt say of me and of my suit,
For I can look for nothing but the worst,
And all my hopes will like a bubble burst,
Since coming from her uncle, much I fear
That she to nothing of the sort will hear."

"Now, then," said Pandar, "what the need to worry
For fear the man might fall from out the moon!
Good Lord, why all this foolish fuss and hurry!
Your time will come, not right away, but soon.
I beg, for God's sake, grant me this one boon—
Let me alone! I know what's best to do!"
"All right," he said, "I leave it all to you.

"But listen, Pandar, one word ere you go!
Don't think that towards my lady I desire
The slightest impropriety to show,
Or to her harm in any way conspire;

For I would rather bear my sorrows dire
Than have her think it was not understood,
That all I mean is meant for her own good."

"And I your backer," Pandar laughed, "O fie!
No need to tell me this, for all say so!
I only wish that she were standing nigh
And hearing all you say. But I must go.
Adieu, be glad and see how things will grow!
In this affair, I'll take the strain and stress,
And yours be all the joy of my success."

Then Troilus began to swell and boast,
A friendly arm o'er Pandar's shoulder cast;
"A fig," he cried, "for all the Grecian host,
For God will help us Trojans to the last!
And here I swear, that ere my days are past,
Many a Greek through me shall suffer sore—
But such like boasting henceforth I deplore!

"Now, Pandar, more than this I cannot say—
Be thou my guide, my confidant, my all,
My life and death both in thy hands I lay!
Help now!" "Yes, not in vain on me you call."
"May God reward you, let what may befall,
For all my fate on you doth now depend,
To make me live or meet my fatal end."

But Pandar, eager now his friend to serve,
To him in few and hasty words replied:
"Farewell, thy thanks I doubt not to deserve!
Have here my pledge, thou shalt be satisfied!"
Then forth upon his thoughtful way he hied,
Considering how he might find time and place
Vicariously to win this lady's grace.

For any man who hath a house to found,
Runs not at once the labor to begin
With reckless hand, but first will look around,
And send his heart's line outward from within,
To see how best of all his end to win.
So Pandar in his contemplation thought,
And planned his work full wisely ere he wrought.

And Troilus, his sloth aside now laid,
Leaping upon his prancing gallant bay,
Upon the field the very lion played.
Woe to the Greek who met with him that day!
And in the town he made such fine display
Of goodly conduct, that in every place
All loved him who but looked upon his face.

For he became, as though but over night,
Most friendly, gentle, generous and free,
Most provident—in short the finest knight
That in his time or any time might be;
Gone now his jests, his boastful vanity,
His lofty ways and all his manner strange,
And all his vices into virtues change.

Now let us cease of Troilus to speak,
Who feels like one who has been wounded sore,
And from his wound still aching and still weak,
But grown more calm, though healed not thus the more,
Submits in patience to the doctor's lore,
Who skilfully his ill investigates—
So Troilus the final end awaits.

BOOK II—
ATTACK

ATTACK

OUT OF these billows black at last we sail,
O Wind, and now the breaking tempests clear!
In this wild sea my skill doth scarce avail
To save the boat that I attempt to steer,
This troubled sea, tempestuous and drear,
Of black despair that Troilus was in;
But lo, the kalends now of hope begin.

O lady mine, O Clio, glorious one,
Be thou henceforth my help, be thou my muse,
To rhyme this book until the whole is done!
All other aid than thine I here refuse,
And therefore lovers all must me excuse,
If pure inventions I do not endite,
But only Latin into English write.

Then give me neither thank nor give me blame
For all this work, for meekly I deny
The fault, if anywhere my tale be lame,
For what my author sayeth, so say I.
And if unskilled in love my pen I ply,
No wonder that, for who would dare assert
A blind man should in colors be expert?

Remember in the forms of speech comes change
Within a thousand years, and words that then
Were well esteemed, seem foolish now and strange;
And yet they spake them so, time and again,
And thrived in love as well as any men;
And so to win their loves in sundry days,
In sundry lands there are as many ways.

If then the situation should arise,
That any captious lover in this place,

Who hears this tale, or reads it with his eyes,
How Troilus sued for his lady's grace,
Should think 'I'd do not so in such a case,'
Or wonder at his words or at his acts,
He may—for me, I merely state the facts.

Travellers to Rome, as on their way they wend,
Hold not one path and not the self-same style;
And in some lands the game would quickly end,
If men made love as we do all the while,
And thus—so openly with glance or smile,
And visits, forms, and pretty speeches, too;
But when in Rome, do as the Romans do.

I doubt if in this land you could find three
Who'd act the same, if they in love should fall;
For what I like, to you may hateful be,
And yet we reach the same end, one and all,
Though some may carve on trees, some on a wall,
As it may chance.—But now where I began,
My story I must hasten as I can.

IN MAY, mother of months, when all is gay,
When flowers, blue and white and red, now grow
Again, as winter's deadly hold gives way,
When balmy breezes o'er the meadows blow
And Phoebus with his brightest beams doth glow
In the white Bull, and of this month the third,
I now shall sing what great events occurred.

Wise Pandar then, for all his helpful speech,
Now felt, himself, the barb of love so keen,
That though he ne'er so well could others teach,
For thwarted love he turned a sickly green;
And all for nothing but this lover's spleen,
To bed he straightway went, and no time lost,
Where all the weary night he turned and tossed.

The swallow Progne, at the break of day,
In song began her still renewed lament
For her changed shape, but still great Pandar lay
Abed, and half asleep, though night was spent,
Until her plaints, as back and forth she went,
How Tereus her sister hence did take,
Aroused the knight and brought him wide awake.

He called aloud, now ready to arise,
Bethinking he must carry out ere noon
For Troilus his promised enterprise,
Reflecting, too, there was a right good moon
For such attempt, and took his way full soon
Unto his niece's palace there beside—
Now Janus, god of doorways, be his guide!

When he had been admitted at the door,
"Where is my lady, pray?" he briskly said;
And in the wake of him who went before,
Straight to her marbled parlor he was led,
Where she sat listening, while her maidens read
Aloud to her the famous ancient rime
Of all the siege of Thebes to pass the time.

"Madam," said Pandar, "and all this company,
How do you do, so busy with your book!"
"Why, uncle, pray come in," responded she,
And up she rose and by the hand him took,
And said, "For three nights now—but let's not look
For bad luck just from that—I've dreamed of you,"
And led him to a chair with great to-do.

"Why, niece, your dreams foretell to you some good,
For one whole year, I reckon," he replied.
"But I'm extremely sorry that I should
Thus interrupt when you are occupied.
What is your book? You can in me confide!
Is it a tale of love? Come, let's draw near!"
"Uncle," she said, "your sweetheart isn't here!"

They laughed, and Cressida stopped to explain,
"This is the tale of Thebes wherein we read,
About King Laius, stricken down and slain
By Oedipus his son, and all that deed.
We were at these red letters, whence proceed
The lines about Amphiorax to tell,
Who sank down in the ground and into hell."

"O yes, I know all that," Pandar replied,
"And all the siege of Thebes and that affair;
In twelve big books it has been versified.
But what's the news? What gossip's in the air?

Put off your gear and show your face all bare!
Lay by your book and let us take this chance
To celebrate the May with song and dance."

"O God forbid!" she cried, "you must be mad!
Is that the way a widow should behave?
Indeed your style of speech is shocking bad,
And almost like a crazy man you rave;
For it would fit me better in a cave
To pray the saints and read their holy lives!
Let maidens go and dance, and youthful wives."

"Well, I could tell," said Pandar with a laugh,
"A tale to make you want to sport and play!"
"Now, uncle dear," she said, "don't tease and chaff,
But tell us, do! Have the Greeks gone away?
I wish the siege would end this very day."
"No, no," says he, "I give my sacred word,
This thing beats any news you've ever heard."

"Heavens alive!" cried she, "what thing is that?
Why won't you tell? Indeed, you stagger me!
I can't imagine, uncle, what you're at!
Some joke, perhaps, that I shall never see,
Till you yourself reveal the mystery.
This talk is too much for my feeble brain,
I can't pretend to follow—please explain."

"Well, no," he said, "I really wouldn't dare,
Because it's not a tale on which you'd thrive."
"And pray why not?" she asked. "You aren't fair!"
"Dear niece," he said, "if this news should arrive
Unto your ears, no prouder woman alive
There could be found in all the town of Troy,
And no exaggeration I employ!"

This made her wonder more and ever more,
And downward thoughtfully her eyes she cast,
For ne'er in her born days had she before
So longed, with longing deep and unsurpassed,
To know a thing, but sighed and said at last,
"Well, uncle dear, of course I shan't insist,
And you can tell me when and what you list."

AND after that with pleasant conversation
And friendly gossip, both of man and maid,
They keep the ball of speech in brisk rotation;
And when in deeper things they start to wade,
As friends will do when they enough have played,
Of Hector's health, the wall of Troy she speaks,
That rod of wrath upon the wicked Greeks.

"He's well," said Pandar, "well as any other,
Thank God, except upon his arm a scratch,
And also Troilus, his younger brother,
To wise and worthy Hector nigh a match,
Such equal virtues to his name attach;
In truth and gentle birth he is not less,
In wisdom, honor, and ample worthiness."

"Good faith!" cried Cressida, "that pleases me!
I don't know where you'd find a better two!
I think it is the finest thing to see
A king's son, who in arms so well doth do,
And he a gentleman, all through and through;
For strength and moral virtue one can find
Not often in a character combined."

"Indeed," said Pandar, "that's the simple truth!
For verily, these princes are a pair,
Hector and Troilus, for all his youth,
That you might safely venture to compare,
So void of vice and full of virtues fair,
With any men that live beneath the sun,
So famous, too, for all that they have done.

"Of Hector there is nothing new to tell;
In all this world there is no better knight,
For of all good he is the fount and well,
One who excels in virtue more than might,
And yet stands strongest in all wise men's sight;
The same of Troilus I dare maintain,
In truth I know not such another twain."

"For Hector," answered she, "I quite agree,
And gladly think as well of Troilus,
For one hears every day how worthily

He bears himself in arms; so generous
He is at home, and ever courteous,
The highest praise and name he hath acquired
From those whose praise is most desired."

"Quite true, quite true," said Pandar in reply,
"For yesterday, as all the town agrees,
It was a sight to fill a wondering eye;
For never flew so thick a swarm of bees
As from him fled the Greeks with quaking knees,
And through the field in every person's ear
There was no cry but 'Troilus is here!'

"Now here, now there, he hunted them so fast,
There was but Grecian blood and Troilus;
For all were crushed or on the ground were cast,
And everywhere you could express it thus,
He was their death, and shield and life for us.
And all that day no man durst him withstand,
The while he held his bloody sword in hand.

"And yet he is the friendliest of souls,
For all his rank, that ever I have seen;
And if he likes a man, he straight enrols
That one in friendly love both firm and keen."
With that he rose with brisk and serious mien,
Prepared to go, and said, "Now I must run
Along." "What for?" said she. "What have I done?

"You really shouldn't be so quickly bored,
Especially with women. Must you go?
Sit down again, if you can time afford
About some business I would like to have you know."
The others all, on hearing her speak so,
Withdrew and at a distance took their stand,
And left them free for all they had on hand.

And when this consultation reached an end
And nothing seemed his going to prevent,
Said Pandar, "On my way now I must wend!
But first, let's dance, and pray won't you relent,
And put aside this sad habiliment?
Why dress yourself in this so mournful way,
When such good luck has chanced to you today?"

"O that reminds me," said she smilingly,
"Shall I not know the meaning of all this?"
"No, I must think it over," answered he,
"For I should never know a moment's bliss
If I should tell and you took it amiss.
And surely I had better far keep still
Than tell the truest truth against your will.

"For niece, by great Minerva, the divine,
And Jupiter, who makes the thunder sound,
And Venus, goddess most especially mine,
No other person on this world so round—
Sweethearts excepted—have I ever found,
That I love more than thee and least would grieve,
And this I think you know and well believe."

"O surely, uncle," said she, "and I'm duly
Grateful for all your long and friendly aid;
To no one have I been beholden truly
So much as you, and yet have less repaid;
You have then little cause to be afraid
That with intention I shall you offend,
And if I have done so, I shall amend.

"But now, dear uncle, let me please beseech,
And as I trust in you, let me insist,
That you leave off this strange mysterious speech,
And tell me clear and plain whate'er you list."
Then Pandar said, though first his niece he kissed,
"I will with pleasure, Cressida my dear,
But take it right, what I shall tell you here."

AT THAT her eyes upon the ground she cast,
And Pandar, with a little cough polite,
Began, "Dear niece, lo, always at the last,
Though some men think their style is stale and trite
Unless with subtle artifice they write,
Beneath their little tricks you always find
The thing that from the first they had in mind.

"And since the point is always at the end,
And since the end is here not hard to see,
Why should I strive my story to extend,
Between old friends like us especially?"

And pausing then as serious as could be,
He gazed intent and long into her face,
And said, "On such a mirror, heaven's grace!"

And to himself he thought, "If what I say
Seems hard to understand or to believe,
Then she will either no attention pay
Or think that I have something up my sleeve;
For simple minds fear all men will deceive,
When they hear something hard to understand,
And so I'll lead her gently by the hand."

His steady looking filled her with surprise,
She wondered why he should be gazing so,
And said, "Good Lord, don't eat me with your eyes!
You've seen me many a time before, you know."
"And better shall," he said, "before I go!
But I was wondering if you were to be
So fortunate, for now we soon shall see.

"For every person hath his happy chance,
If good faith with his fortune he will hold.
But if he turns aside with scornful glance
When fortune comes, unwelcoming and cold,
Then for ill luck he may not fortune scold,
But his own sloth and feebleness of heart,
And he must take all blame from end to start.

"Good fortune, niece, hath lightly come thy way,
If thou wilt but accept it now as thine;
And for the love of God, without delay
Take hold of it, thy share do not decline.
But need I now say more along this line?
Give me your hand, for now it lies with you
To be the luckiest soul I ever knew.

"But let me speak again of my intention—
As I to you have often said before,
There is no living person I could mention
Whose honor and renown I cherish more;
By all the solemn oaths I ever swore,
If you are wroth at this, or think I lie,
I shan't have nerve to look you in the eye.

"Don't be so agitated! Pray, what for?
Don't look as though I meant some harm to you!
The worst is past and there is little more,
I've told the old and now must come the new.
Yet trust in me and you will find me true,
For never sure the least improper thing
Would I to your attention dare to bring."

"Now, uncle dear," she said, "for heaven's sake,
Hurry and tell me what it's all about,
For I am both so scared with fear I quake,
And eager, too, to have the whole thing out!
For be it thing of joy or thing of doubt,
Say on! This agony you must dispel!"
"So will I do," said Pandar, "listen well!

"Now, Cressida, my niece, the king's dear son,
The good, the wise, the worthy, fresh and free,
Who seeks the good and ever so hath done,
The noble Troilus so loveth thee,
That life or death for him you must decree.
So this is all! And as you shall reply,
Consider you will bid him live or die.

"But if you bid him die, you take my life,
For here this pledge, dear niece, I ratify,
That I will cut my throat with this my knife!"
And with these words and tears in either eye,
Pandar went on, "If both of us must die,
And guiltless both, 'twill be a sad affair,
And you alone the blame thereof must bear.

"Alas, that he who is my lord so dear,
That faithful man, that noble, gentle knight,
Who will to nothing but your welfare hear,
That I should see him perish in my sight,
And to his own destruction walk upright,
Hastening to a fate you might prevent!
Alas! that God such beauty to you sent!

"But if you will in careless cruelty
Insist that death at your hands he shall fetch,
A man of high and noble constancy,

As if he were some ordinary wretch,
I tell you all your beauty will not stretch
So far to make amends for such a deed—
And so, before it is too late, take heed!

"Woe to the precious gem that will not glow!
Woe to the herb that harms, but should work weal!
Woe to the power that will no mercy show!
Woe to the pride that treads all neath its heel!
And all ye fair, adorned with beauty's seal,
If therewith pity give not beauty worth,
'Twere pity you should dwell upon this earth!

"Now don't imagine any wrong I mean,
For I would rather thou and I and he
Were hanged, than I should be his go-between,
Or think of aught but what the world might see!
Remember who I am, for shame to me
As well as thee it were, should my endeavor
The least dishonor bring upon you ever.

"Of course you understand I would not bind
You to him in the very least degree;
But merely show yourself a little kind
And in such wise that he can plainly see,
Whereby at least his life assured will be.
Now here you have the whole of my intent,
And all I ever thought or ever meant.

"And sure there's nothing strange in this request,
And not a reason there against to show.
Suppose the worst—that you are fearful lest
Some folk will talk, seeing him come and go.
But I can answer that, and will do so,
That every man, except the weak of mind,
Nothing but friendliness therein will find.

"For who supposes when he sees a man
Going to church, that he expects to eat
The images there! And think how well he can
Comport himself, so heedful and discreet,
A more considerate man you'll never meet.
Besides he won't come here so frequently
But that the whole world might look on and see.

"Such friendship you will find in all this town—
A cloak, no doubt, if folk will use it so.
But as I hope to win salvation's crown,
I've given you the best advice I know.
You can, dear niece, alleviate his woe,
And if so be you can do nothing more,
His death, at least, will not lie at your door."

CRESSIDA weighed these words, so doubtful wise,
And thought, "I'll see just what he's coming to!"
"Now, uncle," said she, "what would you advise?
In your opinion, what is best to do?"
"Well said," he answered, "now I'll tell you true!
Since love for love is but a fair return,
It were great wrong his proffered love to spurn.

"Remember time is wasting every hour
Some share of all the beauty now we see,
And thus, ere age shall all thy charms devour,
Go love, for old, none will have aught of thee!
This saying may a lesson to you be,
'It might have been,' said Beauty, beauty past,
For age will dull all edges at the last.

"The courtly fool is wont to cry aloud
When any woman holds her head too high,
'Long may you live and all ye beauties proud,
Til crowsfeet come to grow beneath your eye,
And in your mirror may you then descry
The face that you shall wear for many a morrow!
I hope and pray for you no greater sorrow!'"

WITH these few words he stopped and bowed his head,
While Cressida with weeping eyes replied:
"Alas, poor me! I wish that I were dead!
No honor in this world doth now abide;
For how shall I in strangers e'er confide,
When he who seemed to be my trusty friend
Would have me do what he should reprehend.

"In very deed and truth, I should have thought,
If I had loved, through chance unfortunate,
Him or Achilles or Hector, or shown aught
Of love to man of high or low estate,

Such conduct you would sternly reprobate,
And would me ever after discommend!
This faithless world, who may on it depend!

"Is this your fateful joy and happiness?
Is this your counsel, this my lucky chance?
Is this the care that you to me profess?
Is all thy pomp of speech and circumstance
But to this end? O Pallas, let thy glance
Now rest on me with sympathetic eye,
For I am so astounded I shall die!"

SHE paused and sighed with sorrow deep and sore,
And Pandar asked, "Is that all you can say?
Well, I'll be blessed if e'er again your door
I darken, if you doubt me in this way!
I see how little heed to us you pay,
Or to our death! Yet if it may but be
That he is saved, let fall what will on me!

"O cruel God, O most avenging Mars!
O Furies three of hell, on you I cry!
The door that to this house the entry bars
May I ne'er pass, if I meant harm thereby!
But since I see my lord and I must die,
Here let me say it with my final breath,
That wickedly you do us both to death.

"But since it pleases you to see me dead,
By Neptune, god of all the ocean free,
From this time forth I scorn all daily bread
Till with my eyes my own heart's blood I see,
For I shall end my days as soon as he!"
And then he started off like one distraught,
But with restraining hand his cloak she caught.

And though she almost passed away for fear,
For she at best was easy to affright,
At all the horrid things that she must hear,
And saw how deadly earnest was the knight,
And thought besides it maybe was all right,
And that she might stir harm up all the more,
Relenting just a bit and sighing sore,

She thought, "How often comes catastrophe
For love, and in such strange and dreadful way,
That men will treat themselves with cruelty.
And if here in my presence he should slay
Himself, there'd be a frightful price to pay!
What men would think of it, I do not know—,
Perhaps I'd better go a little slow."

Aloud with heartfelt sigh she then replied,
"Ah, Lord, what trouble on me thou hast laid!
For my good name is periled on one side,
And thereagainst my uncle's life is weighed.
But for all that, perhaps with heaven's aid,
Some way to save my name I can devise
And your life, too." With that she dried her eyes.

"The less of two misfortunes I must choose,
Yet would I rather yield to Troilus,
With honor, than my uncle's life to lose.
Will you be satisfied to leave it thus?"
"Indeed yes," Pandar smiled, victorious.
"Well then," said she, "I'll see what I can do.
I shall my heart against my will construe,

"Yet will in no way raise his hopes too high,
For love a man I neither can nor may
Against my will, yet otherwise shall try
Honorably to please him day by day;
Nor had I once to all this thing said nay,
Were not my head so full of fantasies;
But stop the cause, you stop the whole disease!

"But here I make a solemn protestation,
That if you in this matter too far go,
Then certainly, for your nor his salvation,
Though both of you together die, and though
Each man alive become my deadly foe,
'Twill be the end of things twixt him and me."
"O certainly," said Pandar, "I agree."

"But tell me," said he, "can I trust in you
That all that you have promised to me here,
That all of this you faithfully will do?"

"Why yes," she said, "why not, my uncle dear?"
"And that you won't draw back from foolish fear
So that forever I shall have to preach?"
"Why no," she said, "what need of further speech?"

THEY talked of many things with right good cheer,
Till finally she said, "Before you go,
There's one thing, uncle, I should like to hear,
How of this matter you came first to know.
And is it spread abroad?" "By no means, no!"
"Is he well versed," she asked, "in these affairs?
Do tell—I might be taken unawares!"

Then Pandar answered with a little smile:
"I see no reason why I shouldn't tell!
The other day—'twas just a little while—
Within the palace garden, near a well,
Troilus and I in conversation fell
About some new and promising design
With which the Grecian force to undermine.

"And then we started in to jump and leap,
And cast our darts in practice to and fro,
Till Troilus said he would go and sleep,
And laid him down where soft the grass doth grow,
And I went farther off and left him so,
Until as I was walking there alone,
I heard him fearfully begin to groan.

"And then I stalked him softly from behind,
And heard all he was saying, clear and plain,
And just as I recall it now to mind,
Of love he spoke, and this was his refrain:
'O Lord, have pity now upon my pain!
Though I have been a rebel in intent,
Now, mea culpa, Lord, I do repent!

"'O God, who ever holdest in possession
The ends of things, in justice all comprising,
In thy good will accept my meek confession,
And send me penance at thy own devising;
Yet let not grief, from black despair arising,
Exile my spirit far away from thee,
But be my shield in thy benignity.

"'For truly, Lord, the one who stood in black,
So deeply with the glancings of her eye
My heart on its foundations doth attack,
I know that from the wound I'm doomed to die.
And yet the worst is this, I can't reply,
And hotter grow the glowing coals so red,
When covered o'er with ashes pale and dead.'

"And then he laid his head upon the ground,
And muttered something which I couldn't hear,
And then I went away without a sound,
So that I might pretend to re-appear,
And soon came back again, and standing near,
I cried 'Awake from out this slumber deep!
It's plain that love cannot disturb your sleep!

"'You sleep so sound I scarcely can you wake!
Who ever saw, forsooth, so dull a man?'
'Let lovers,' said he, 'love till their heads ache,
But let me get along as best I can!'
And though his face was wan beneath its tan,
Yet he put on a cheerful countenance,
As though all ready for a song or dance.

"So it continued, till the other day
It chanced that I came wandering all alone
Into his chamber, and found him where he lay
Upon his bed, and man so sorely groan
I never heard, but why he thus should moan
I did not know, for soon as he saw me,
He stopped his lamentation suddenly.

"You well may think, this made me grow suspicious,
And drawing near, I found him weeping sore,
And as I hope for grace from acts flagitious,
I never saw a sight that touched me more;
With all my wit and all my wisest lore,
This man I scarcely from his death could keep,
And even now my heart for him doth weep.

"God knows, not since the day that I was born,
Had I such need to any man to preach,
Nor ever was there man so deeply sworn
Ere he would tell me who might be his leech!

But bid me not rehearse again his speech,
And all his melancholy words repeat,
Or I shall drop and faint here at your feet.

"To save his life, and with no other thought,
Except no harm to you, thus am I driven!
And for God's love, who all the world hath wrought,
See thou that life to both of us be given.
And now to you in full my heart I've shriven,
And since you see that it is pure and clean,
You know full well that I no evil mean.

"I pray to God, successful may you be,
Who such a fish hath caught without a net!
If you are wise, as you are fair to see,
Well in the ring then is the ruby set.
You two will make the best pair ever yet!
And heaven bless the day which well assures
That you are his as much as he is yours."

"Oho! I did not say that," answered she,
"Such talk as that will help things never a deal."
"O niece," said Pandar, "pray you, pardon me!
For though I merely spoke out as I feel,
I meant it well, by Mars with helm of steel!
So be not angry with me, dearest niece!"
"O well," she said, "for this time I'll make peace."

AND then he took his leave and homeward bent
His way, with progress made well satisfied,
And Cressida got up and straightway went
Into her private chamber close beside,
And still as a stone, she sat her down and tried
Each word that he had said to bring to mind,
And all interpretations of them find.

And she was somewhat troubled at the thought
Of all she'd heard and done, but still when she
Had weighed it well, it seemed that there was naught
To justify so great timidity;
For though a man with love near bursting be,
Nothing compels a woman to respond,
Unless, indeed, she should of him grow fond.

And as she sat alone, reflecting thus,
The noise arose of skirmishers without,
And men cried in the street, "Lo, Troilus
Hath put the coward Greeks to flight and rout!"
And all her household ran up with a shout,
"O let us see! Throw up the lattice wide!
As he goes home, he through this street will ride!

"There is no other way here from the gates
Of Dardanus where they've let down the chain."
And then he came, with all his battle mates,
All riding slowly in a double train;
And that it was his lucky day 'twas plain,
A day on which things turn out as they should,
And even bad luck turns at last to good.

Troilus rode upon his good bay steed,
All armed, except his head, in richest gear;
The wounds upon his charger still did bleed,
As slowly down the street the band drew near.
O what a noble sight did then appear!
Like Mars himself for battle all arrayed,
Troilus led the warlike cavalcade.

He was the picture of a warrior knight,
A man of greatest prowess in all ways,
For bold in mind, he strove with equal might
In deeds that won a universal praise.
It was pure joy upon this knight to gaze;
So fresh, so young, with such vitality,
He was, in truth, a heavenly sight to see.

His helm was hacked in twenty different places,
So that it hung by just a slender thread;
His shield was cut by strokes of swords and maces,
With arrows buried in it to the head,
Where horn and sinew made for them a bed.
And loud the people cried, "Here comes our joy,
And with his brother, great defense of Troy!"

And Troilus a little blushed for shame,
When thus he heard the people shout and cry;
To watch him was as good as any game,

How soberly he downward cast his eye;
And Cressida, intent on all to spy,
Felt in her heart a softly sinking motion,
And sighed, "Has someone given me a potion?"

And at this thought she blushed a rosy red,
Bethinking her, "This is the very he
Who loves me so, so hath my uncle said,
That he will die, unless help comes from me!"
And then in modest fear that he might see,
She drew back from the casement window fast
As Troilus and all his people passed.

And then in mind she canvassed up and down
The count of all his gracious qualities,
And all his rank and all his great renown,
His wit, his figure, all his knightly ease,
But that he loved her, most of all did please;
And then she said, "This man to death to do,
'Twere pity, if his mind and heart are true."

NOW envious folk might make objection thus:
"This was a sudden love! How might it be
That she so quickly should love Troilus
At sight?" Why, such things happen frequently,
And if you doubt, just look about and see!
For all things slight beginnings first must know
Before to full completion they can grow.

For mark, not in the twinkling of an eye
She gave her love to him, but did incline
To like him first, and I have told you why,
And afterward, his qualities so fine
Made deepest love within her heart to mine,
And only then, for proper service done,
And not by sudden glance, her love was won.

Recall also that Venus, well arrayed,
Within her seventh house just then doth go,
With all kind aspects at that time displayed
To help poor Troilus in his deep woe;
And she was not in any case a foe
To Troilus from his first natal hour,
Whereby in love he had the greater power.

Let Troilus in peace his ways now go,
And let us turn to Cressida, shamefast
And pensive, sitting with her head bent low
And trying solitary to forecast
What courses she should follow at the last,
If Pandar persevering for his friend
Should push this suit unto the final end.

Then in her heart she started to debate
Of this affair, as I have to you told,
And over this and that to hesitate
Till she had twisted it in many a fold;
And now her heart was warm, now was it cold,
And some of what she thought I shall relate,
Though far too long were all of her debate.

And first she thought that Troilus she knew
At least by sight, and all about his birth,
So high she said, "Of course it would not do
To think of love, with one of such high worth,
But still 'twould be an honor, but in mirth
And in all innocence, for me to deal
With one like him, and mayhap for his weal.

"I don't forget he is my sovereign's son,
And since he seems in me to take delight,
If I all his advances harshly shun,
He might be angry with me, and with right,
Whereby I might fall in a still worse plight.
Would that be wise if I his hate incurred,
When I might have his love for just a word?

"In everything there should be moderation,
For though one might forbid all drunkenness,
One could not say that men through all creation
Should never drink—'twere folly, nothing less;
And since for me he feels all this distress,
No reason I should scorn him and despise,
That is, if he behaves in goodly wise.

"But well I know, and so does everyone,
That he in all affairs is most discreet,
And boaster, too, most surely he is none,
Nor idle tales or secrets would repeat;

But that's a point on which I need not treat,
For he shall have no chance to boast of me,
Or hold me by such bonds of secrecy.

"But now suppose the worst should come about
And men should gossip of his love for me,
Need that upon my name cast any doubt?
Can I stop him from that? Why, he is free!
I know, and every day I hear and see,
That men love women, yet no leave have they,
And when they want to stop, they can and may!

"Of course I know he is a splendid catch,
To get whom women all would do their best,
If no dishonor thereto did attach;
For he by far surpasses all the rest,
Save Hector only, who is worthiest,
And yet his life is subject to my glance!
But such is love, and such my lucky chance!

"That he should love me surely is no wonder,
For I am not so simple but I know
(Though naturally I say this only under
My breath) that I am fair, as women go,
Fairer than most, though I myself say so,
But plenty here in Troy will say the same;
If he thinks well of me, who can him blame?

"I am my master, too, here at my ease,
Thank God for that, and with a fair estate,
Right young and free to do just as I please,
With husband none to say to me 'Checkmate!'
Or worry me with troublesome debate.
For husbands all are full of jealousy,
And masterful, or hunting novelty!

"What should I do? Shall I not have some fun?
Shall I not even love, if so inclined?
Why not, I'd like to know! I'm not a nun!
What if my heart a resting place should find
Upon this knight, the best of all mankind,
If I preserve my honor and my name,
I see no cause in that of harm or blame!"

NOW like the sun in March which shines out bright,
Though oft the March sun, too, doth hide his face,
For though the winds may put the clouds to flight,
Their courses soon again the clouds retrace,
So now a cloudy thought began to race
Across her heart, o'erspreading like a pall
Her sunny thoughts with shadowy thought withal.

The thought was this, "Alas, since I am free,
Should I now love and risk my happy state
And maybe put in bonds my liberty?
What folly such a course to contemplate!
Am I not satisfied to see the fate
Of others, with their fear and joy and pain?
Who loveth not, no cause hath to complain.

"For lovers ever lead a stormy life,
And have done so since loving was begun,
For always some distrust and foolish strife
There is in love, some cloud across the sun.
Then nothing by us women can be done,
But weep in wretchedness and sit and think,
'This is our lot, the cup of woe to drink!'

"And slanderous tongues, they are so very quick
To do us harm, and men are so untrue,
And once they're satisfied, they soon grow sick
Of ancient love and look for something new!
But when all's done, then what can women do!
These men at first their love like mad will spend,
But sharp attacks oft weaken at the end.

"Full often it hath been exemplified,
The treason that to women men will show;
And that's the end, when such a love hath died,
For what becomes of it, when it doth go,
No living creature on this earth can know,
For then there's nothing left to love or spurn;
What once was naught, to nothing doth return.

"And if I love, how busy must I be
To guard against all idle people's chatter,
And fool them that they see no fault in me,

For true or not, to them it doesn't matter,
If but their lying tales amuse or flatter;
For who can stop the wagging of a tongue,
Or sound of bells the while that they are rung!"

But when her cloudy thoughts began to clear,
She countered, "Nothing venture, nothing gain!
All things must have their price, or cheap or dear."
This thought brought dark forebodings in its train,
And hope and fear were linked in endless chain,
Now hot, now cold, and thus between the two
She started up, still doubtful what to do.

DOWN stairs along the garden paths she went,
And calling to her there her nieces three,
They rambled through the garden's whole extent,
Flexippe, Tarbe and Antigone,
A charming and a pleasant sight to see;
And others of her women came along,
And in the garden made a merry throng.

The place was large, and all the alleys railed,
And shaded well with flowery boughs, all green
With branches new, nor gravelled paths there failed
On which she walked, two nieces dear between,
The while Antigone, with cheerful mien,
Began to sing a Trojan lay, so clear
It was a heavenly joy her voice to hear:

"O GOD of Love, to whom I e'er have been
A humble subject, true in my intent
And will, through thee, O Love, I hope to win
What joy shall ever to my heart be sent!
For I opine that no one has been meant
By thy good grace a happier life to lead
Than I, whose joy by thee has been decreed.

"O blissful God, so happy is my state,
No creature on this earth, with creatures rife,
Could equal me in love or be my mate;
For Lord, with neither jealousy nor strife,
I love one who is eager with his life
To serve me, tireless and unrestrained,
And with a love by no dishonor stained.

"For he whose mastership I here confess,
The ground of truth and virtue's looking-glass,
Apollo for wit, the rock of steadfastness,
The root of good, whose joys all joy surpass,
Who makes all sorrow wither as the grass—
I love him best, and so doth he love me;
Success to him, whoever he may be!

"Whom should I thank but thee, thou God above,
That now to bathe in bliss I may begin?
Have here my thanks, O Lord, that I may love!
The happy life is this that I dwell in,
The refuge here from every vice and sin!
Such virtue loving to my heart doth lend
That day by day I feel my life amend.

"And anyone who says that love is wrong,
Or slavery, then he is nothing less
Than envious, or in his wit not strong,
Or lacking power to love for crustiness;
And folk who talk of hardship and distress,
But slander love and nothing of him know;
They talk, but they have never bent his bow.

"For is the sun the worse in its own right
Because some man, for weakness of his eye,
May not endure its radiance so bright?
Or love the worse, though some against it cry?
No weal is woe that sorrow can outvie,
And people in glass houses should be wary,
And specially of throwing stones be chary.

"But I with all my heart and all my might,
As I have said, with loving unsurpassed
Will love my love, my true and precious knight,
To whom my soul hath grown so firm and fast,
And his to me, our love shall ever last;
Though once with love I dreaded to begin,
Now well I know no peril lies therein."

WHEN thus her song to happy end she brought,
Cressida spoke up, "Dearest niece," she said,
"Pray tell me who this pleasant ditty wrought?"
She gave no name but answered thus instead,

"Madam, the goodliest maid and highest bred
Of all maids in this pleasant town of Troy,
Who lived her life in honor and in joy."

"So it would seem, to judge her by her song,"
Said Cressida, and therewith paused and sighed,
"I wonder, doth such joy in truth belong
In love as by such ditties seems implied!"
"O yes," Antigone with rapture cried,
"For all the folk that dwell in mortal state
The joy of love in full could not relate.

"But 'tis not every humble creature knows
The perfect bliss of love! Most surely not!
For foolish men will foolish things suppose;
Most think it's love if only they are hot!
But ask the saints if you would know the lot
Of those in heaven, for they alone can tell,
And ask the devil if it's foul in hell."

Cressida to this said nothing in reply,
Observing but, "It's getting on toward night,"
Yet all these words within her memory lie,
Imprinted on her heart all clear and bright;
And now indeed of love she feels less fright
Than she had done, for now love sits at ease
Within her heart, with greater power to please.

THE crown of day and heaven's brightest eye,
The foe of night (I merely mean the sun),
Westward and downward now began to hie,
For he the course of one full day had run,
And all things bright were turning drear and dun
For lack of light, while stars came out in scores,
And Cressida betook herself indoors.

And when at length time came to go to bed
And all the folk had left the house who ought,
To go to sleep she felt inclined she said,
And soon her women to her bed her brought;
And there in silence lay she still and thought
And thought, but all her thoughts I can't delay
To tell, and you can guess them anyway.

Upon a cedar green a nightingale,
Under the chamber wall near where she lay,
Full loudly sang against the moonlight pale,
A song perhaps of love, as birds well may,
For love alone could make a song so gay;
And listening long, this loving song sank deep
Within her heart before she fell asleep.

And as she slept, she dreamed, and dreaming saw
A wondrous eagle, feathered snowy white,
And from her breast he tore with curving claw
Her heart, and then she saw a stranger sight;
Where hers had been, he put his heart forthright,
At which no fear she knew, nor pain nor smart,
And forth he flew, with heart exchanged for heart.

SO LET her sleep, and let us now give heed
To Troilus, who to the palace rides
From that same skirmish on his prancing steed,
And to his chamber goes, and there abides,
But sends his courier, and two or three besides,
To look for Pandar, whom they straightway sought
And found and to the palace quickly brought.

Pandar came running in at once and said,
"O what a day! What Trojan ever yet
Has had such storms of swords upon his head
As Troilus! It made you hot, I'll bet,"
And laughed and joking said, "Lord, how you sweat!
But come, it's late, and time you should clean up."
"All right," said Troilus, "let's go and sup."

In haste they went, in haste they also supped,
Then back again and so prepared for bed,
Sending away all who could interrupt
The confidential things that might be said;
And Troilus, whose very heart-strings bled
Until he heard what news his friend would bring,
Cried out, "Now tell me, shall I weep or sing?"

"O hush!" said Pandar, "let me go to sleep!
And you do, too! You have no need to worry,
But choose if you will dance or sing or leap.

Just trust in me and don't be in a hurry.
To tell the truth, she's in as great a flurry
As you are in, and near as resolute,
If only you don't slacken in pursuit.

"For your affair I have so well begun
And carried on, that on this very day
Her loving friendship I for you have won
And her good faith against it she doth lay—
Your woe in one leg's crippled anyway!
But why should I a longer discourse hold,
For all that you have heard, to him he told.

And as the flowers, closed by cold at night,
Hang drooping on their stalks all limp and low,
But straighten up against the sunshine bright
And in their proper way expand and grow,
Troilus lifted up his eyes just so
And said, "O precious Venus, goddess mine,
All honor to thy grace and power divine!"

To Pandar then he held out both his hands,
And said, "Good sir, all that I have is thine!
For I am healed, and broken are my bands!
A thousand Troys, if thousand Troys were mine,
Could not together happily combine
To give me such a joy, for lo, my heart
So swells, it seems in fragments it must part.

"What shall I do? And how shall I survive?
And when again shall I my sweetheart see?
The tedious time away how shall I drive
Until you bring back further news to me?
'Tis easy quite to say 'Go slow,' but he
That's hanging by the neck in mortal pain
Has no desire hanging to remain."

"Now, now," said Pandar, "by the love of Mars,
You know that all things have their proper season,
And that the night immediate action bars;
But if you'll listen to a little reason,
I'll go the earliest hour that she agrees on;
In some things you must do just what I say,
Or on some other man your charges lay.

"For heaven knows, I ever yet have been
Ready at call, nor ever to this night
Have I held back, for though my wit be thin,
I've done my best, according to my might.
Do as I say, and it will be all right.
But if you won't, to me it's all the same,
Though in that case, I shall not bear the blame.

"I know that thou art wiser far than I,
But were I in the selfsame fix as thou,
I know the very plan that I would try.
With my own hand I'd go and write her now
A letter, telling her exactly how
The love of her had driven me near crazy.
Now stir yourself and don't be slack or lazy.

"And I myself will with your letter go,
And at the time that I am with her there,
In all your gear to make the bravest show,
Upon your courser to her street repair,
As though it were upon some chance affair,
And you will find us at a window-seat,
So shall I manage, looking in the street.

"And if you want, give us a brief salute,
But when you do, of course at me you'll glance,
And then ride on, as though on some pursuit
That called you hence. Don't stop, by any chance!
Just take it steady, and on your way advance,
And after you are gone, to her I'll turn
And tell her things will make your ears both burn.

"Respecting that letter, you are wise enough,
Only I wouldn't write in too high style,
Or spin fine arguments obscure and tough.
Don't write too neat, and use a little guile—
Let tear stains blot your words once in a while;
But if you find a word you think is clever,
Use it but once, don't harp on it forever!

"For though a harper were the best alive,
And had the best harp in the world to play,
And played it best with all his fingers five,
If he but touched one string or sang one lay,

However sharp his nails were filed away,
His music would but make men dull and sad,
And only when he stopped would they be glad.

"And don't mix things that do not harmonize,
In love and medicine the same note strike,
But always use the style that best applies
To what you say, so that it seems life-like;
For if a painter painted finny pike
With asses' feet and headed them like apes,
He'd be no artist but a jack-a-napes."

TROILUS thought this counsel very wise,
But timid lover that he was, replied,
"Pandar, alas, I see what you advise,
But I'm afraid to write, I must confide!
Such letters I have never seen nor tried,
And if she took amiss what I might say,
Goodnight for me—'twould be my fatal day!"

"Don't balk," said Pandar, "go ahead and write,
And let me with your letter to her go,
And by the Lord and his eternal might,
I'll have an answer soon that I can show
From her own hand. But if you won't do so,
I give it up. And heaven help the chap
Who tries to help you out of your mishap!"

"O Lord," his poor friend answered, "I give in!
Since you insist, I'll get up now and write!
May God help you your journey's end to win,
When, as and if my letter I endite!
Minerva, O thou goddess fair and bright,
Grant me the wit my letter to devise!"
Then down he sat and wrote her in this wise.

His only lady first he did her call,
Life of his heart, his joy, his sorrows' cure,
His bliss, and many other terms that all
Good lovers use their ladies to assure;
And then with humble words and with demure,
He begged that she would show to him some grace—
Of course to tell you all I haven't space.

Then next he begged in meek and humble fashion
That she would cast at least a pardoning eye
On what he dared to write, and said his passion
Left him no choice, except he wished to die,
Nor stopped with that at piling it on high;
Himself of small account he did profess,
And added that his deeds were worth still less,

And begged her to excuse his lack of skill,
And said it was because he feared her so,
And harped upon his subjugation still,
And on his sufferings too deep to show,
And said that they would even greater grow,
And then goodby, with pledges new and old,
And so his letter ready was to fold.

The ruby in his signet with his tears
He bathes, and when he hath it neatly set
Upon the wax, its impress there appears;
A thousand times then he did not forget
To kiss his missive with his kisses wet,
And said, "O letter, what a joy for thee!
Tomorrow thou my lady dear shalt see."

THE letter in the morning Pandar took
To Cressida, as soon as he could start.
"Are you awake," he cried, "let's have a look!"
And then he laughed and joked, and said, "My heart
Remains so fresh, for all love makes it smart,
I cannot sleep on such a May-time morrow!
I have a jolly woe, a lusty sorrow!"

Cressida greeted him with some surprise,
Eager to know, but also with some fear
Why he came there, she questions and replies,
"What lucky wind has brought you over here
So early in the morning, uncle dear?"
Tell us your jolly woe and your mischance!
What progress are you making in love's dance?"

"As ever," he said, "I'm limping far behind!"
At which she laughed as if her heart would burst.
"I hope," said Pandar, "you will always find

Me cause for mirth! But listen to me first—
There's come a stranger to this town accursed,
A Grecian spy, and he great tidings brings—
I thought you'd like to hear about these things.

"Let's go into the garden, you and I,
I'll tell you privately this latest news."
Then arm in arm, down from her chamber high
They walk into the garden cool, and choose
A quiet path where no one hears or views
The things they say or do, and thus concealed,
Pandar the precious letter straight revealed.

"He who is altogether yours," said he,
"Petitions you must humbly for your grace,
And sends to you this letter here by me.
Regard it well at fitting time and place,
And with your pen some goodly answer trace,
For now I tell you once for all and plain,
He cannot longer live in so great pain."

The letter she beheld, but stood quite still,
And took it not, till anger drove out fear,
And then she loudly cried, "Nor script nor bill,
For love of God, bring never to me here
From such a source. And also, uncle dear,
For my good name have more regard, I pray,
Than for your friend. What need I further say?

"Pray tell me, do you in your heart believe,
For all your guileful words and cunning speech,
That I could properly this note receive,
Or put in practice what you seem to preach,
And both of you so earnestly beseech,
And not wreck all my good repute and fame?
Take it away, I bid in heaven's name!"

"Why, Cressida," he said, "you are quite droll!
Is this the first you've heard of this, I wonder!
Let Jove to depths infernal damn my soul,
Or strike me down with sudden stroke of thunder,
If for the town whose walls we're sitting under,
A harmful word to you I'd ever carry!
Your conduct seems to me extraordinary!

"But I suppose you think like all the rest,
That he deserves the least who most does try
To serve and aid you with his very best!
But though you reck not if he live or die,
And all my good intentions you deny,
You shan't refuse." And then he seized her gown
And in her bosom thrust the letter down.

"Now then," he said, "this note I dare you throw
Away, that folk may see your grand display!"
"O, I can wait," she said, "until you go!"
And then she smiled and added, "Uncle pray,
Such answer as you will to him convey,
For truly, uncle, I shall write no letter."
"I'll dictate," said he, "if you think that's better."

She laughed at this and said, "Let's go and dine!"
And he agreed, assured the worst was past,
And said, "Dear niece, for love I peak and pine
So much, that every other day I fast!"
And told his jokes, some new, some old recast,
And made her laugh till she was out of breath,
And thought that she would laugh herself to death.

When they had come together to the hall,
"We'll dine," she said, "in just a minute or so,"
And her attendants coming at her call,
She said that to her room she'd have to go,
And there, as Pandar very well did know,
However pressing any other need,
Her letter first she would be sure to read.

She read it word by word and line by line,
And on the whole she thought it pretty good,
And put it up and then went in to dine.
Pandar apart in deep reflection stood,
And she came up and took him by the hood,
"Aha," she said, "a penny for your thought!"
"Have what you will," he said, "I'm fairly caught!"

And then they washed and set them down to eat,
And after dinner, Pandar with design,
Drew near the window looking on the street.
"Whose house is that," he asked, "decked out so fine,

A little further down across from thine?"
"Which house," she answered, drawing near to see,
And knew it well, and told its history.

And there they stayed and talked of this and that,
Both sitting down within the window bay,
But after much such unimportant chat,
And when her women all were gone away,
Then Pandar turned and said, "Well, niece, I say,
How was the letter, good or just so-so?
How does he write? I'd really like to know."

At that she blushed a quick and rosy red,
But merely answered, "H'm! Of course you would!"
"Now you must write a fair reply," he said,
"I'll sew your letter up all tight and good,
Across the middle, if you say I should,
And if you want, just make your letter small,
But let your uncle fold and sew it all."

"Perhaps I might," she murmured soft and slow,
"But if I should, I don't know what to say!"
"O niece," said Pandar, "such things quickly grow!
At least your grateful thanks you can convey,
And say some words his trouble to repay.
Indeed it's only decent courtesy
To grant at least so much to him and me."

"O dear," she said, "I hope it's quite all right!
I never thought to write a man a letter,
It really puts me in a nervous fright!"
Into her room she went to work the better,
And there alone her heart she doth unfetter
Out of the prison of disdain a while,
Striving a fitting letter to compile.

And what she wrote, in brief I mean to tell,
So far as I have heard or understand;
She thanked him first that he of her thought well,
But said she really could not take in hand
A serious answer to his chief demand,
But as a sister, if she could him please,
She'd gladly do her best his heart to ease.

She closed it then, while Pandar mused alone,
Beside the window looking on the street,
And brought it in, and sat upon a stone
Of jasper by him on a cushion seat,
With beaten gold embroidered, fair and neat,
And said, "I've never done a harder thing
Than write this letter which to you I bring!"

With thanks he took the letter and replied,
"You know from things with heavy heart begun,
Come happy endings. Niece, you may take pride
That you by him have not been lightly won,
For in the tale of sayings true, the one
That says the truest runs, 'Impressions light
Are always lightly ready to take flight.'

"But you have played the tyrant nigh too long,
And made your heart a hard thing to engrave;
So now relent and don't bear down too strong,
(Of course appearances we still must save),
And henceforth in a gentler way behave,
For manners cold or hard will soon or late
Turn every liking to dislike and hate."

AND as they sat thus, friendly and confiding,
Lo, Troilus, along the lower end,
Came up the street with escort slowly riding,
And by this very house they must ascend
As to the palace on their way they wend.
Pandar at once beheld this fine array,
"Look, niece," he said, "who's riding up this way!

"Don't go away—he sees us I suppose—
'Twill look to him as though you feared pursuit!"
"No, no," she said, as red as any rose.
Troilus, riding by with grave salute,
And changing hue, and timidly and mute,
A gentle glance or two upon her cast,
Nodded to Pandar, and on his way he passed.

O Troilus, he was a goodly sight,
In goodly form he was that happy day!
He looked, and was in truth, a manly knight!

No need to stop and tell of his array,
And only one small thing I need to say,
That Cressida was favorably impressed,
By person, manner, look, and all the rest.

So well indeed, and by his gentleness,
That never since the day that she was born,
She felt so deep for any man's distress
As now for him upon this fateful morn!
To tell the truth, she hath picked up a thorn
At which she may full long and vainly pull!
God grant all hearts with such thorns may be full!

And Pandar, who was standing there near by,
Began to strike, feeling the iron hot.
"Dear niece," he said, "I wish you would untie
For me this simple little lovers' knot!
If this man guiltless through some woman got
His death, because her heart was hardened so,
Were it well done?" "I'd say," she answered, "no!"

"And you'd say right," with ardor Pandar cried,
"With proper spirit you are now imbued.
Lo, forth he rides!" Says she, "Well, let him ride!"
"O come," said Pandar, "don't be such a prude!
Enough of this reluctant attitude!
Give him a hopeful word just for a start,
This holding off but frets and grieves the heart!"

With that the argument was on again!
"With what you say," she said, "I can't agree;
"Just think how all of Troy would talk! And then,
It's far too soon to grant a liberty!"
To this alone she would consent, said she,
To love him at a distance, as she might,
If he could be content but with her sight.

But Pandar thought, "O that will never do!
She must get over such a foolish notion;
This matter can't run on a year or two."
But for the present he was all devotion
And thought it best to raise no great commotion,
And seeing all was well, at fall of eve,
He rose and said goodby and took his leave.

And on his homeward way full fast he sped,
And felt for very joy his heart must dance.
Troilus he found, extended on his bed,
Most lover-like, deep in a lover's trance,
Twixt hope of good and fear of evil chance,
And Pandar bursting in, began to sing,
A signal meaning, "Something good I bring."

"Who's buried here in bed," he cried, "so soon?"
A faint voice issued forth, "It's only me."
"Who? Troilus? Now by the sacred moon,"
Said Pandar, "get thee up and come and see
A wondrous charm that has been sent to thee,
To heal thee from all irksome grief and pain,
And make thee joyful, brisk and spry again."

"O yes, a miracle," said Troilus.
Then Pandar could no longer hold it back,
And said, "The Lord today hath favored us!
Bring here some light to look on all this black!"
Then joy and fear in turn made sharp attack
On Troilus, as he his letter read,
For in her words he found both hope and dread.

But in the end he took it for the best,
And thought that in her letter she had said
Some things at least on which his heart could rest,
Although between the lines they must be read;
And so to optimistic views thus led,
And trusting, too, in Pandar as his friend,
His deep despair began a bit to mend.

AND as we may ourselves on all sides see,
The more the wood or coal, the more the fire;
As with increase of probability
There often comes an increase of desire;
As oaks from acorns grow and mount up higher,
So now this lover's flame more brightly burned,
His head by just one little letter turned.

And so it came to pass that day and night,
Troilus began to hunger more and more,
And as his hope increased, with all his might
He strove to put in practice Pandar's lore,

In writing to her of his sorrows sore;
Each day the effort new he made
In letters which by Pandar were conveyed.

To all proprieties he paid good heed
That to a lover in his case pertain;
And as the dice fell and as fate decreed,
His days were days of joy or days of pain,
Yet with his writing he did still proceed,
And echoing to the answers that he had,
His day took color, either glad or sad.

And Pandar ever was his great recourse,
And of his woes the sole recipient;
In him he found a never-failing source
Of aid, for Pandar could not rest content
To see his friend so languish and lament,
And ever in his mind he cast about
To find some fruitful way to help him out.

"My lord and friend," he said, "and brother dear,
It hurts me sore to see you take on so!
But do look up and be of better cheer,
For I've a little scheme I'd like to show,
Which I devised a day or two ago,
Whereby I'll bring you to a certain place,
And in her presence you can plead your case.

"I have no doubt this point is known to you,
But those who are expert in love declare
There's nothing like a personal interview
To help along a lagging love affair.
Just make her of your state of mind aware,
For every gentle heart it must impress
To see and hear the guiltless in distress.

"Perhaps you think, 'Though it may well be so,
That Nature doth constrain her to begin
To have some sort of pity on my woe,
Yet Will replies, "Thou shalt me never win!"
So doth her spirit rule her heart within,
That though she bend, she stands firm on her root.
What good, then, does all this to my poor suit?'

"But on the other hand, the sturdy oak,
On which have been delivered many a blow,
Receives at last the happy falling stroke,
And all at once the whole tree down doth go,
Like heavy rocks or millstones falling low;
For things of weight come down with swifter flight
When they descend, than do things that are light.

"A reed that lowly bows before the blast,
After the wind again will lightly rise.
But not so when an oak-tree down is cast—
Of course you see what this exemplifies.
One should take pleasure in an enterprise
Of pith and moment placed beyond a doubt,
Though it took time to bring it all about.

"Now, Troilus, I have a slight request,
A little thing that I must ask of thee.
Which of thy brothers doth thou love the best
Within thy heart's most secret privacy?"
"Deiphebus it is," at once said he.
Said Pandar, "Ere another day shall end,
Unwittingly he shall thee well befriend!

"Leave it to me! I'll do the best I can!"
Then to Deiphebus he took his way,
Who was his lord and he his faithful man,
And more than this, long-standing friends were they,
And there arrived, he said his little say:
"I beg of you, my lord, that you will be
Friend to a cause that nearly touches me."

"O, quite!" Deiphebus replied. "You know,
There's not a man within this mortal sphere
To whom a favor I'd more gladly show,
Troilus excepted, whom I hold most dear.
But first perhaps you'd better let me hear
What's weighing now so heavy on your mind,
And then the remedy we'll try to find."

PANDAR his troubles thus doth then proclaim:
"My lord, there is a lady here in Troy,
My niece, and Cressida is her good name,

Whom certain men are trying to annoy,
And for themselves her property enjoy.
It is for her your aid I now beseech,
As I have told in plain and simple speech."

"Is she," he asked, "this lady in distress,
Of whom you speak in such a formal way,
My old friend Cressida?" Said Pandar, "Yes."
"Why, then," he cried, "there's nothing more to say!
For you can count on me in any fray
To champion her with sword or shaft or spear,
And this I'll say for all her foes to hear.

"But since you know the case, just tell me how
And what to do." Said Pandar, "Well, let's see!
If you, my gracious lord, would do me now
The honor to request my niece that she
Should come tomorrow, and here publicly
Present her case, I'm sure her enemies
Would hesitate to press their wicked pleas.

"And one thing more you might consent to do—
I wouldn't ask, except for her great need—
If some of your brothers could be here with you,
'Twould greatly help the case that she will plead
To have them all in her support agreed.
For with your aid and that of other friends,
She'll check her foes and thwart their wicked ends."

Deiphebus, who was by nature kind,
And glad to be a friendly instrument,
Replied, "It shall be done! And I can find
A better plan, which should her well content!
How would it be if I for Helen sent
To join with us? I'm sure that she will come,
And count for two, with Paris 'neath her thumb.

"And Hector, who to me is lord and brother,
No question but that he her friend will be!
For I have heard him, one time and another,
Commend her, and in such a high degree,
That she will need no assiduity
To win him to her side. Her only task
Will be, whatever she may want, to ask.

"And you yourself might speak to Troilus,
On my behalf, and ask him here to dine."
"O gladly," Pandar said, "I shall do thus!"
He took his leave and straight as any line,
He hastened forth to further his design,
To Cressida, whose dinner just was finished,
And straight began with ardor undiminished.

"O Lord," said he, "O what a way I've run!
Look, niece! Just gaze at what a sweat I'm in!
I hope I'll have your thanks for all I've done.
You know that Poliphete, that man of sin,
Is planning a new action to begin,
And open up fresh charges in your case?"
"I? No!" she cried, and grew pale in the face.

"What, will he never cease me to torment
And do me wrong? Alas, what shall I do!
For him alone I wouldn't care a cent,
But there's Antenor and Aeneas, too,
Both friends of his—in all, a wicked crew!
But I am weary, uncle, of this strife;
I'd give up all to have a peaceful life—

"A very little will suffice for us!"
"No, no," said Pandar, "I won't have it so!
But I've been talking with Deiphebus
And Hector, and with other lords you know,
And Poliphete will find in each a foe.
I pledge my word, this case he shall not win,
No matter when or what he may begin."

And as they sat considering this affair,
Deiphebus himself, most graciously,
In his own person came to see her there,
And ask the favor of her company
To dine next day. To this she did agree,
As proper was her lord thus to obey,
And he expressed his thanks and went his way.

THEN Pandar left her with her thoughts alone,
For now on Troilus he must attend,
And while his friend sat still as any stone,
He told him all the tale from start to end,

How unawares Deiphebus would lend
His aid, and said to him, "Now if you can,
Is time to stir yourself and play the man!

"Speak up tomorrow, beg, beseech and pray,
And don't hold back for fear or modesty!
The time has come when you must say your say.
Don't lose your nerve, and you'll see what you'll see,
For as they say, the truth shall make thee free!
But something seems to stick still in your mind,
And what it is, I'll wager I can find.

"Perhaps you think, 'How shall I do all this?
For by my looks the folk will soon espy
And quickly guess that something is amiss,
And than they should do so, I'd rather die!'
But this is folly, and I'll tell you why;
For I've a scheme, it's something really bright,
To keep you safely out of all men's sight.

"To your dear brother's house I bid you go,
And say that you have come a while to stay,
And that by illness you've been troubled so,
But think a change may drive it all away.
Then go to bed, and when they ask you, say
You feel too ill and weak to dine or sup,
But lie right there, and wait for what turns up.

"And say your fever is cotidian,
And daily comes and goes at its own pleasure;
Just play the invalid the best you can,
And sick he is whose grief is out of measure.
Go, now! The time is past for idle leisure;
It's nerve will win the day in this affair.
Just keep your head and say goodby to care."

"In truth," said Troilus, "there is no need
To counsel me a sickness to pretend,
For I am sick in very fact and deed,
So sick it well may be my fatal end."
"That's good," said Pandar, "no time need you spend
On how to counterfeit the sick man's lot,
For one who sweats, is taken to be hot.

"Just hold you steady in your snug retreat,
And I the deer before your bow shall drive."
They parted then, though soon again to meet,
And each with other ready to connive.
Now Troilus is glad he is alive,
With Pandar's plan he is quite well content,
And to his brother's house at night he went.

With cordial welcome there he was received,
Deiphebus expressing sympathy,
And at his illness all were deeply grieved;
They covered him with bed-clothes carefully,
But still he seemed as sick as he could be;
He kept in mind what Pandar to him said,
And naught they did could budge him from his bed.

Before they from the sick man's room descend,
Deiphebus requested him to do her right
And be to Cressida a help and friend,
And Troilus agreed with words polite,
And said he would with all his will and might—
Of all requests this was as needless one
As bid a wild man leap and jump and run.

RECALLING next day where she was to dine,
Helen the queen, the famous and the fair,
Informally and some time after nine,
Doth to her kindly brother's house repair,
Just to a little family dinner there,
And took it as a usual event,
Though God and Pandar knew what it all meant.

Cressida, unsuspecting, brought along
Antigone and Tarbe, sisters two—
In fact the diners numbered quite a throng;
But I don't mean to pass here in review
The names of guests and all they say and do,
For you can guess their greetings and their chatter,
And we'll proceed to more important matter.

Deiphebus his guests doth entertain
With most delicious foods, the very pick,
But now and then, "Alas," was his refrain,

"That Troilus in bed is lying sick!"
Yet to this theme he did not always stick,
But often spoke of things more bright and cheery,
To keep his honored guests from growing weary.

And Helen, too, was really very nice
In warm expression of her sympathy,
And each one had some medical advice
To give—"I think the best treatment would be"—
"This charm indeed I recommend to thee"—
But to this lore that one made no addition
Who thought, "'Tis I could be his best physician."

And then his praises they began to sing,
As folk will do when someone has begun;
A thousand variations there they ring
Upon this theme, and praise him to the sun,
"What he can do, there's mighty few have done!"
And all the flattering things of him they say,
Pandar confirms in most emphatic way.

Cressida heard, although she took no part,
And every syllable she kept in mind;
Though grave her look, she laughing was at heart,
For who alive would not great comfort find
To think she could about her finger wind
A knight like that! But now too long I dwell
And must proceed the end of this to tell.

THE time came from the table to arise,
And thus they stood about, while each one spoke
By chance of one or other enterprise,
Till on the conversation Pandar broke
And said, "Deiphebus, to all this folk,
May I now beg you somewhat to declare
Of Cressida's unfortunate affair?"

And Helen, holding Cressida's right hand,
Spoke first. "O, do!" with sympathy she cried,
As side by side together there they stand.
"By Jupiter, an evil fate betide
The wretches who to injure you have tried!
For sure, if I have anything to say,
They'll see good reason to regret the day."

"You state the case," remarked Deiphebus
To Pandar, "since you know it all so well."
"My lords and ladies all, it standeth thus,
No need," he said, "too long on it to dwell"—
Then rang them out a story like a bell
About this Poliphete, and made it stretch
So far, they felt like spewing on the wretch.

They all abused him, each worse than the other,
And right and left the scoundrel they did curse:
"He should and shall be hanged, were he my brother!"
"And that's too good, if anything were worse!"
But why should I a lengthy tale rehearse?
For each and all assured her in the end,
They'd do their best and be her staunchest friend.

"O Pandar," Helen said, "pray tell to us,
Is my good lord and brother—Hector, I mean—
Informed of this affair? And Troilus?"
"Why, yes," he said, "but that reminds me, queen!
It seems to me, if Troilus can be seen,
It might be best, that is, if all assent,
If she herself saw him before she went.

"For he will have the matter more at heart,
If he should know the lady in the case,
And by your leave, right for his room I'll start,
And let you know within a second's space,
If he can hear her story in that place."
And in he ran and whispered in his ear,
"God bless thy soul, I've brought thy pillow here!"

This joke drew forth a smile from Troilus,
And Pandar, lacking cause for long delay,
Went back to Helen and Deiphebus,
And said, "If she can come now right away,
But with no crowd, then come, he says, she may,
And he will hear what it is all about,
As long as he is able to hold out.

"But since you know the chamber is but small,
And people crowding in might make it hot,
I would not have the blame on me to fall
That I had added to his heavy lot,

No, not for all the arms and legs I've got.
Perhaps we'd better try some other day;
But that, of course, is all for you to say.

"But still, I think 'twill be the better plan
For none to go in first except you two,
And maybe me, who in a second can
Rehearse her case better than she can do;
And when you leave him, she can follow you
And ask for his support at no great length—
I don't think this will overtax his strength.

"Then, too, since she is strange, he might exert
Himself for her, but not for his own kin,
Besides I'm almost sure he will revert
To secret plans for helping Troy to win
Her way from out the siege that we are in."
And all unwitting of his deep intent,
Without ado to Troilus they went.

And Helen, always gently soft and sweet,
Began with him to chat and gently play,
And said, "O, we'll soon have you on your feet!
Now, brother, for my sake, be well, I pray!"
And on his shoulder doth her white arm lay,
And strives with gentle art as one who fain
Would somewhat ease him on his couch of pain.

"We've come," she said, "to ask some help from you,
My brother dear Deiphebus and I,
For love of—O, and so does Pandar, too,—
To be a friend to one whom we hold high,
To Cressida, who no one can deny
Has been much wronged, and Pandar over there,
Her case and situation can declare."

THEN Pandar once again his tongue must file
To tell his tale convincingly yet brief;
When this was done, thinking a little while,
Troilus said, "When I have some relief,
Of all my duties that shall be the chief,
In Cressida's behalf to intervene."
"And all success to you!" replied the queen.

"Perhaps," said Pandar, "if you can her see
And say goodbye before she hence doth go"—
"O yes, of course she must," responded he,
"If she will be so good as to do so!"
Then turning, said, "To you I want to show,
Deiphebus and Helen, sister dear,
A matter of importance I have here,

"And ask you what course seems to you the better,"
And fished out from his bed a document,
And handed it, together with a letter
Which Hector to him recently had sent,
Whether a sentence of death he should prevent,
I know not whose, and with some agitation
He begged them give it their consideration.

Deiphebus first hastens to unfold
The letter, and then together with the queen
Downstairs he goes, a conference to hold,
And in a little quiet arbor green,
They talk the matter out themselves between,
And for an hour's span, or less or more,
This document they read and on it pore.

SO LET them read, and let us turn again
To Pandar, now so jubilant to find
How well all went. He hastened out and when
He came into the room where they had dined,
He cried, "To all of you may heaven be kind!
But come, my niece, Queen Helen waits for you,
And both our gracious lords are waiting, too.

"Just take with you our niece Antigone,
Or whom you will—or rather come alone,
The less the crowd the better. Come now with me,
And when to them your gratitude you've shown,
With Troilus you briefly may condone,
And take your leave of him when you think best,
Though we must not disturb too long his rest."

Of Pandar's dark design all innocent,
Cressida said, "Come, uncle, let us go!"
And arm in arm out of the room they went,

With all decorum, dignified and slow,
And Pandar said, as they passed down the row,
"Good friends, your patience we shall not abuse,
If for a time yourselves you will amuse.

"But don't forget what folk are there within
And one of them, God help him, in what plight!"
"Dear niece," he murmured in her ear, "begin
But gently with this man and do him right,
And by the Lord who grants us life and light,
And by the crowning power of virtues twain,
Let him not lie here in this mortal pain!

"Defy the devil! Keep Troilus in mind,
And in what state he lies! Don't sit so tight!
A chance once lost, you never again will find.
You'll both be glad when you give up the fight.
There's no suspicion yet, however slight,
About you two, and count it time well won
When all the world is blind to what is done.

"In hesitations, false starts and delays,
Men read deep meanings from a wagging straw.
For you at last are coming merry days,
Yet you hold back and timidly withdraw,
And of vain gossip stand in such great awe,
You waste the time you never can recover.
Have pity now upon this sorrowing lover!"

But now I bid you, lovers far and near,
Regard poor Troilus and his sad state,
Who lay and all this whispering could hear,
And thought, "O Lord, I soon shall know my fate,
To live in love, or else to die in hate!"
His time was come now for her love to pray,
And, mighty God, what shall he do and say!

BOOK III—
SURRENDER

SURRENDER

O happy light, of which the beams so clear
Illume the third expanse of heaven's air,
Loved of the sun, of Jove the daughter dear,
O Love's Delight, thou good and fair,
In gentle hearts abiding everywhere,
Thou primal cause of joy and all salvation,
Exalted be thy name through all creation!

In heaven and hell, on earth and salty sea,
All creatures answer to thy might supernal,
For man, bird, beast, fish, herb and leafy tree,
Their seasons know from thy breath ever vernal.
God loves, and grants that love shall be eternal.
All creatures in the world through love exist,
And lacking love, lack all that may persist.

Mover of Jove to that so happy end,
Through which all earthly creatures live and be,
When mortal love upon him thou didst send,
For as thou wilt, the power lies with thee
Of ease in love or love's adversity,
And in a thousand forms is thy descent
On earth, in love to favor or prevent!

Fierce Mars for thee must subjugate his ire,
All hearts from thee receive their fates condign;
Yet ever when they feel thy sacred fire,
In dread of shame, their vices they resign,
And gentler grow, more brave and more benign;
And high or low, as each in his rank strives,
All owe to thee the joys of all their lives.

Houses and realms in greater unity,
And faith in friendship thou canst make to grow.

Thou understandest likings hard to see,
Which cause much wonder that they should be so,
As when in puzzlement, one seeks to know,
Why this loves that, why she by him is sought,
Why one and not the other fish is caught.

From thee comes law for all the universe,
And this I know, as all true lovers see,
That who opposeth, ever hath the worse.
Now, lady bright, in thy benignity,
Help me to honor those who honor thee,
And teach me, clerk of love, that I may tell
The joy of those who in thy service dwell.

True feeling in my naked heart infuse
That in my hands thy glory grow not less!
Calliope, thy voice let me now use,
For great my need! Now all my effort bless,
Who strive, in praise of Venus, this gladness
Of Troilus in fitting words to sing!
May God all lovers to such gladness bring!

NOW all this time poor Troilus still lay,
Conning his lesson most industriously;
"I think," he planned, "just so and so I'll say;
Thus will I lead her my deep love to see;
This word sounds good, 'twill help in some degree,
And this by all means I must not neglect"—
And so on, all to much the same effect.

Hearing her come, how he begins to quake,
And how he sighs, with sighings short and quick,
While Pandar by the sleeve his niece doth take,
And peeping at him through the curtains thick,
He cries, "Now God have mercy on the sick!
See who has come a visit here to pay!
Behold the fatal cause of all this fray!"

With tearful weeping Pandar's eyes o'erflow,
"Oh, Oh!" groans Troilus, most groanfully,
"How bad I feel, O Lord, no one does know!
Who all is there? It's hard for me to see."
"O, sir," said Cressida, "Pandar and me."
"What, you, my dear! Alas that I can't rise
And do you honor in a fitting wise."

He raised him up, but she at once drew nigh,
Her two restraining hands on him to lay.
"O, please," she cried, "for my sake please don't try!
(O, what was that I had in mind to say!)
Sir, here I come for two things, if I may,
To thank you first, then ask you as my lord
Your favor and protection to accord."

HEARING his lady to him humbly pray
For lordship, Troilus from shame near dead,
Had not a single word to her to say,
For he could think of none to save his head;
But suddenly he flushed a crimson red,
And all the clever things he'd counted on,
Fled from his mind, completely lost and gone.

Cressida understood this well enough,
For she was wise, and liked him none the less
Because he was not pert or quick and rough,
Nor yet so bold he lacked all humbleness.
But when his shame had passed its first excess,
His words, as in my way then can be told,
And as the old books say, I shall unfold.

With strange and trembling voice, from simple dread
Abashed, and blushing now from ear to ear,
But changing often too, now pale, now red,
To Cressida, his chosen lady dear,
Submissive standing at his side so near—
Lo, all he said when he his lips could part,
Was, twice, "O mercy, mercy, my sweetheart!"

He paused, and when he tried again at length,
His next word was, "God knows that I have been
All yours, with all I have of wit and strength,
And shall be yours, by him who saves from sin,
Until they dig my grave and put me in!
And though I'm slow of speech and hesitate,
My love by that you must not estimate.

"So much at present, O thou woman true,
I may declare, and if these words displease,
With my own life I'll make the payment due,
If by my death I may your wrath appease,

And bring your heart again to rest and ease.
For now that you have let me have my say,
I care not how or when I pass away."

Such manly sorrow in his bosom burned,
Tears from a heart of stone it would have drawn,
And Pandar wept as though to water turned,
And nudged his niece anon and yet anon,
And said, "Was ever man so woe-begone!
For God's sake, bring this matter to an end,
And slay us both, and on your ways then wend!"

"What's that?" cried she, "I know not for my part
Just what it is you're asking me to say!"
"What's that?" he said, "just show you have a heart,
Nor this poor creature pitilessly slay!"
"Well, then," she said, "I'd ask him, if I may,
To tell me clearly what he has in mind,
For never yet his meaning could I find."

"Just what I have in mind, O sweetheart dear!"
Cried Troilus. "That thou so fair to see,
But with the beamings of thine eyes so clear
Sometimes will turn a kindly gaze on me,
And that, besides, to this thou wilt agree
That I in root and branch, and every way
In truth, may serve thee well from day to day,

"As rightful lady and my chief resort,
With all my wit and all my diligence,
And as you will, may have from you support,
According as you judge my competence—
Or death for any disobedience—
And that this honor you to me will show,
To seek my aid in all things high or low,

"And let me be your servant sworn and true,
Humble and secret, patient in endeavor,
Eager to find occasions fresh and new
To serve, and in my service slacken never,
And what you will and bid receiving ever
With good intent, however sore I smart—
Lo, this I have in mind, my own sweetheart!"

"INDEED," said Pandar, "that's a hard request,
And something any lady would deny!
My dearest niece, as I look to be blessed,
If I were God, I'd let you pine and die,
If honor, honor were your sole reply
To such a man, so faithfully approved,
By whom the hardest heart might well be moved!"

Though Cressida would not be pushed too fast,
Yet in a manner not at all severe,
A glance or two on Troilus she cast,
And answered soberly and plain and clear,
"Saving my honor, which I hold most dear,
With all formalities observed and kept,
This man into my service I accept,

"Beseeching him, for love of God, that he
By all the truth and honor of his birth,
As I mean well, may mean as well by me,
And ever hold my honor at high worth.
And if I may increase his joy and mirth,
In all good will, I shall thereto assent;
Take courage then, and cease your sad lament.

"But still this warning note I yet must sound—
A king's son though you be in all men's sight,
In love I shall be only so far bound
As would in any case be just and right;
And if you do amiss, I shall requite
With blame, yet also as you knightly serve,
Shall cherish you and praise as you deserve.

"In short, dear heart, and now my worthy knight,
Rejoice and put aside your fear and dread,
For truly I shall strive with all my might,
For bitter days to give you sweet instead,
And if through me to joy you can be led,
For each past woe you shall receive a bliss"—
And sealed her words with an embrace and kiss.

FELL Pandar on his knees, and up his eyes
To heaven cast, with hands extended high.
"Immortal God," he cried, "within the skies,

Cupid I mean, whom all men glorify,
And Venus, too, rejoice with melody!
Methinks in all the town, with no hand swinging
To mark this miracle, the bells are ringing!

"But soft! we'll wait until another day,
Because Deiphebus will come back soon—
And hark, I hear them coming up this way.
But, Cressida, some morn or afternoon,
And Troilus, too, at season opportune,
A meeting at my house I shall arrange,
The remnant of your pledges to exchange,

"When you can ease your troubled hearts at leisure;
And let us see then which shall bear the bell
In boasts of love which love alone can measure,
For there you'll both have time your tale to tell."
"How long," asked Troilus, "am I to dwell
In this suspense?" "As soon as you get up,"
Said Pandar, "come to dine with me or sup."

With these words, Helen and Deiphebus
Appear, as they the topmost stairs ascend,
And now again deep groans from Troilus
Burst forth, as he bethinks him illness to pretend;
But Pandar says, "It's time for us to end
Our visit, niece, so take leave of all three,
And let them talk, and you come on with me."

She said goodby in quite the proper way,
And they in turn, in polished manner, too,
The pleasant compliments of parting pay;
When she had left and closed the interview,
They still commenced her with praises new,
Her wit, her charm and all her general style,
And Troilus listened with an inward smile.

Now to her palace let her wend her way
While we go back to Troilus in bed;
About the letter he had naught to say
That Helen and Deiphebus had read,
And wished that they would go, and soon he said
He thought perhaps it might for him be best
To try to sleep and get a little rest.

And Helen kissed him then and said goodby,
Deiphebus likewise his leave must take;
But Pandar soon, as straight as he could fly,
Came back, a couch beside his friend to make,
And Troilus and he, both wide awake,
Through all that confidential night there lay,
For they had many pressing things to say.

When all had left the room except these two,
And firmly shut and barred was every door,
Their conversation they began anew,
And Pandar left his couch upon the floor,
And on the bed he sat, and now once more
Began to speak in his accustomed way
To Troilus, as I shall to you say.

"MY LORD most worshipful and brother dear,
God knows, and thou, what pain and grief I bore
To see thee languishing through all the year
For love that ever the longer grew the more!
Thus I with all my might and all my lore
Did ever since my time for you employ
To bring you back from sorrow into joy,

"And have so far my plannings carried out
That you to gain your end are in good way.
But there is nothing here to boast about,
And know you why? With shame I must it say,
For you I have begun a game to play,
The like of which I'd do for no one other,
Although he were a thousandfold my brother.

"That is to say, I've made myself for thee
Half jest, half earnest, such a go-between
As oft twixt man and maid the world doth see.
You know yourself what kind of thing I mean;
For thee I've made my niece, so pure and clean,
Such confidence and trust on thee bestow
That henceforth all just as thou wilt shall go.

"But God omniscient here I witness take,
For private ends in this I have not wrought,
But only strove thy sufferings to slake,
Which well nigh fatal were, or so I thought.

But, brother dear, remember that you ought,
In every manner, keep her free from blame,
And always strive to save her honest name.

"For well you know a woman's reputation
Among the people is a sacred thing,
And never man, I dare make affirmation,
A charge of wrong on her could justly bring;
But now the dreadful thought my heart doth wring,
That she should be my niece, so dear to me,
And I her uncle and her pimp should be.

"And were it known that I, through set design,
Had put my dearest niece in such a way
To follow thee and be all wholly thine,
Why, all the world would cry aloud and say,
That no such treachery for many a day
Was in this fashion planned and done,
And she be lost, and for thee nothing won!

"And so before a further step we take,
No matter what befall, I ask again
For secrecy, for hers and for my sake;
Do not disgrace me in the eyes of men!
And be not wroth at me if now and then,
I beg for privacy in this affair,
For well you know how urgent is my prayer.

"And think what woes of old have come to pass
From boastful speech, and how today men lead
Their lives in griefs that burden and harass,
From hour to hour, for that same wicked deed.
And in the wisest clerks you well may read
This proverb, useful to the old and young,
'The highest virtue is to hold your tongue.'

"And if I would not now abbreviate
Diffusiveness in speech, I could almost
A thousand ancient tales to you relate
Of women lost through false and foolish boast.
Such proverbs you yourself must know a host;
All boastful blabbers are but fools forsooth,
Even if what they say seems like the truth.

"One tongue, alas, hath often made to mourn
And caused full many a lady bright of hue
To cry, 'Alas the day that I was born!'
And many a maid her sorrow to renew;
And yet the things are twisted all askew
Of which men boast, if they were brought to proof;
Boasters by nature are from truth aloof.

"A boaster and a liar, all is one!
For now suppose a woman granteth me
Her love, as to no other she hath done,
And I am sworn to sacred secrecy,
And then I go and talk to two or three,
Then I'm a boaster and a liar both,
For I have broken all my plighted troth.

"You see right well how much they are to blame,
Such sort of folk—or scamps would be more pat—
Who boast of women, even by their name,
Who never promised them nor this nor that,
Nor knew them any more than my old hat!
I ask you, is it any wonder then
That women fear to get involved with men?

"I don't say this especially of you—
I hope you're not in need of all I've said.
I'm thinking of the harm that people do
By heedlessness, and not by malice led;
For well I know no woman need to dread
The vice of boasting in a man of sense;
The wise learn from the fools to shun offence.

"But to the point! Now my good brother dear,
Keep all these things that I have said in mind,
And ponder well. But now, be of good cheer,
And doubt not at the proper time to find
Me true, for I shall work in such a kind
That you therewith shall be well satisfied,
For all shall be as you yourself decide.

"I have no doubt of thy integrity,
And therefore all this task I undertake.
Thou knowest that thy lady grants to thee

A day on which thy settlement to make!
And now goodnight! I cannot keep awake.
And pray for me, since heaven doth thee bless,
God send me death, or make my sorrow less!"

NOW who could tell one half the jubilation
Which Troilus within his heart then felt,
Hearing the end of Pandar's protestation!
The wounds that grief unto his heart had dealt
Began for joy to vanish and to melt,
And all his multitude of sightings sore
Dispersed and fled away forevermore.

As when the woods and hedges everywhere,
Which through the winter waited dead and dry,
Reclothe themselves in green, so fresh and fair,
And all the folk rejoice with spirits high,
The same thing now in him you might descry;
His heart with joy to blossom so began
That in all Troy there was no happier man.

Then Troilus his eye on Pandar cast,
Most soberly, yet in a friendly way,
And said, "O friend, remember April last,
For I am sure you can't forget the day,
How nearly mortal sorrow did me slay,
And how you long and earnestly did press
Me there to tell the cause of my distress?

"You know how long to speak I then forbore,
Although you were the man I trusted best,
And nothing hindered me then to declare
The truth to you. Now tell me, I request,
Since nothing of my love I then confessed,
How durst I babble in the general ear,
And tremble now, with no one by to hear?

"But by the God omnipotent I swear,
By him who deals to every man his fate,
And if I lie, may not Achilles spare
To cleave my heart, that I shan't divulgate,
Though I should live forever, soon or late,
A word of this, or hint to anyone,
For all the gifts of God beneath the sun.

"The rather would I end my days withal,
Fettered in prison cell would rather be,
In wretchedness where filthy vermin crawl,
In Agamemnon's harsh captivity;
And this in all our temples faithfully,
By all our Gods tomorrow I will swear,
And you can go along and witness bear.

"That thou hast done so very much for me
That all thy service I can ne'er repay,
I understand quite well, although for thee
I died a thousand times and more a day;
But as thy slave, and what more can I say,
Upon thy wish and will I shall attend,
Till death shall bring my life unto its end.

"But let me now with all my heart beseech
That you assign me no such attribute,
As I might fairly gather from your speech,
That you supposed that all my honest suit
Was but a bawdy thing of ill repute.
I'm not a scholar, but I'm not a fool,
I've learned a thing or two outside of school.

"A man who this affair should undertake
For gold or profit, call him what you will!
But what you've done, you did for pity's sake,
Through goodness of your heart and not for ill.
Regard it so, for men of any skill
All know that the distinctions subtle are
Between two things a good deal similar.

"And here's another thing that I declare
To wipe from all your act the shameful blot;
Behold my sister Polyxena fair,
Cassandra, Helen, or any of the lot,
Though she be fair with never a stain or spot,
Just tell me which of these you'd like to be
Your very own, and leave the rest to me!

"But since thou thus hast helped me in this wise
To save my life, and not for hope of meed,
So, for the love of God, this great emprise
Carry thou out, for now there is much need;

In high and low, in every single deed
All thy commands I faithfully will keep,
And so goodnight, and let us go to sleep."

THUS each with other was well satisfied,
No better friends in all the world could be;
The next day, early up and dressed, each hied
Him to his regular activity;
And Troilus, although he longed to see
The one on whom depended all his joy,
Took heed all right precautions to employ,

And every reckless action to restrain
With manly will, and each unbridled look;
There was no man alive could entertain
The least suspicion, such good care he took
That none might nose him out by hook or crook.
He held himself as lonely as a cloud,
From policy, and not that he was proud.

And all this time of which I now relate,
He daily strove with valor and with might
The service high of Mars to cultivate
In deeds of arms befitting a true knight;
And on his couch when darkness followed light
He lay, and thought how he might serve
His lady best, and thus her thanks deserve.

I will not say, although his couch was soft,
That he in heart was fully at his ease,
Or that he turned not on his pillow oft,
Nor longed to grasp what was too far to seize.
Such lonely nights have little power to please—
So I've been told,—and so thought he maybe;
I note it as a possibility.

But this is sure, in order not to stray
Too far among reflections manifold,
He saw his lady, yet not every day,
And spoke with her, although too rash or bold
They neither were, and always strove to hold
Themselves in hand, for each one felt the need
With proper care and caution to proceed.

And when they spoke, they spoke so quick and brief,
With great reserve and with oppressive fear,
(For folk are prone to jump at some belief,
And strain to gather something through the ear),
That all would think that nothing was so dear
To them as this, that Cupid should them send
An opportunity their speech to end.

But though they spake but little or spake naught,
His spirit was so tuned in every deed,
It seemed to her he knew of all her thought
Without a word, so that there was no need
To caution or for aught to intercede;
For so it seemed that love, though come so late,
To all their joy had opened up the gate.

In short, to bring the matter to a close,
So faithfully he did on her attend,
That high in his dear lady's grace he rose,
And twenty thousand times or more on end
She thanked the Lord that she had such a friend,
Who could conduct himself in all his ways
So well, he merited the highest praise.

In truth she found him so discreet withal,
So secret ever and obedient,
She felt he was to her a very wall
Of steel and shield from fear or discontent;
And when she saw how nicely all things went,
She felt she had no need to be so wary—
I mean, of course, no more than necessary.

And Pandar, ready still to feed the fire,
Was ever diligent and close at hand.
To please his friend was now his sole desire,
He urged him on, was ready at command
To carry letters, or for him to stand,
When Troilus was busy or away—
In short, the perfect confidant to play.

But if you think that I should now relate
Each word of Troilus, each hope and fear,
The little nothings, sweet and intimate,

That he meant only for his lady's ear,
I couldn't do it if I took a year;
To tell you every passage of his wooing
Would be a labor scarcely worth the doing.

I do not find that ever anyone
In telling such details has been minute—
'Twould be appalling if it were all done!
In letters thousands of verses I compute
They wrote, on which my author is quite mute;
He was too sensible and wise to try
To write all lovers say, and so am I.

But to the great result! As things stood thus,
These two in concord and in peace complete,
These lovers Cressida and Troilus,
Were well content in all this time so sweet,
Except that only rarely they could meet,
And had so little time their joys to tell,
I now proceed to say what next befell.

GOOD Pandar, striving still with all his might
To lead this matter to a happy end,
Thought how to bring unto his house some night
His niece so dear, and his still dearer friend,
That at their leisure they might there attend
To this great love by which they both were bound,
And finally a fitting time he found.

He made his plans with great deliberation,
Providing for all things that might avail
To help them realize their expectation,
However great the toil this might entail,
And worked it out so that it could not fail,
And that for anyone through it to see,
Would be a sheer impossibility.

To fool all folk his plan was well designed,
The spoil-sports and the gossips, all the same;
He had no doubts, for all the world is blind,
In such affairs, the wild ones and the tame!
And now the timbers ready are to frame!
There's nothing lacking now except to know
The hour at which to his house she should go.

And Troilus, who all this plotting knew,
And patiently in silent waiting lay,
Had also planned with care what he would do,
And also, for excuse, that he would say,
If he were not about some night or day,
That to a certain temple he would go,
His duty to the deity to show,

And solitary there would watch and wake,
If some sign from Apollo he might see,
Or might behold the holy laurel shake,
Or hear Apollo speaking from the tree,
To tell him when the Greeks would homeward flee;
And therefore let him as he will pretend,
And pray Apollo bring all to good end.

And now we're coming to the point right soon!
For Pandar up and with no great ado,
But when there was a changing of the moon
And lightless is the world a night or two,
And when the clouds foretold a rain in view,
To Cressida, his niece's house he went,
And you well know the whole of his intent.

When he arrived, in his accustomed way
He joked and jested at his own expense,
But finally he paused and made display
Of earnestness and of great exigence,
And said for no excuse and no pretence,
He'd let her off, but come she must that eve
To supper at his house by her good leave.

At this she laughed and in excuse replied,
"It's raining, look! So how then could I go?"
"That's nothing," said he. "Just let me decide.
You've got to come—I will not take a no!"
And so at last they left the matter so,
For he had whispered softly in her ear,
"Don't come if you won't, but for it you'll pay dear!"

But she was not quite ready to give way,
And asked if maybe Troilus was there.
"O no," he said, "he's out of town today!
But, niece, I say, supposing that he were,

You have no slightest cause for fear or care,
Indeed a thousand times I'd rather die,
Than have folk on him at my house to spy."

EXPLICITLY no one has set it down,
Just what she thought when Pandar told her so,
That Troilus was that day out of town,
If Cressida believed his tale or no;
But that she went with him to sup we know,
At least, as he so urgently besought,
No matter what she knew or what she thought.

But nevertheless she did again beseech,
Although to go she had no hesitation,
That he forget not foolish people's speech,
Who dream what never was in all creation,
And that he give this full consideration;
"For, uncle," said she, "since in you I trust,
Take heed, for follow where you lead I must."

To do all this he swore by sticks and stones,
And all the gods that high in heaven dwell,
Or let him be, said he, both skin and bones,
As deep as Tantalus in lowest hell
Where Pluto reigns! What is there more to tell?
All thus arranged, he rose and took his leave,
And she to supper came when it was eve,

Along with certain of her household men,
And with her charming niece Antigone,
And others of her women, nine or ten.
Who now was glad? Who other can it be
But Troilus, who stood where he could see,
Right through a little window in a room,
Where he till midnight hid in lonely gloom,

To all the folk save Pandar quite unknown?
But to the point! When she had come at last,
With all her friends, as I before have shown,
Her uncle with his arm about her cast,
Together with his guests to supper passed,
And when they all were seated happily,
The dainties served there were a sight to see.

When from the supper table they arose,
At ease in mind and heart was man and maid,
And each for her his freshest stories chose,
While Pandar his most sparkling wit displayed.
He sang; she played; he told the tale of Wade,
But everything at last must have an end,
And she prepared her homeward way to wend.

THOU Chance, executrix of each man's weird!
O Influences dwelling in the sky!
All under God, our fates by these are steered,
Though we poor brutes the cause cannot descry;
For though she said that homeward she would hie,
The Gods had willed it in another way,
And willy-nilly, there she had to stay.

The curving moon, with her two horns all pale,
And Saturn, Jove and Cancer so united
That all the rains of heaven now assail
The earth, and all these ladies were affrighted,
Who by the smoky rain were thus benighted;
But Pandar only laughed at them, and cried,
"'Tis fine for ducks and ladies now outside!

"But now, good niece, I hope that you will please
Accept my humble hospitality,
As well for mine as for your greater ease,
And all remain here overnight with me.
Pray let my house for once your own house be;
For if you went out now, I'd feel to blame,
And take it as an insult and a shame."

And Cressida, who saw how matters stood
As well as anyone, had naught to say,
For since the flooding rain had come for good,
She thought, "I might as well, if I must stay,
Accept the matter in a cheerful way,
And have his thanks, as grumble and remain,
For home we cannot go just now, that's plain."

"That's very kind," she said, "my uncle dear,
And if you really wish, it shall be so.
We're glad to have the chance of staying here.

'Twas but a joke when I said I would go."
"I thank you, niece," he answered, bowing low,
"Joking or not, the simple truth to tell,
I am relieved that with me you will dwell."

SO FAR, so good! Then they began anew
The conversation in a merry strain,
But Pandar kept the main point still in view,
And he to get them soon to bed was fain.
"Good Lord," he said, "this is a mighty rain!
It's just the weather for a good long sleep!
Let other things until tomorrow keep!

"And, niece, I have a place for you to stay,
Right here, where we shan't be too far asunder,
And where you shan't hear in the slightest way
The noise of raining or the din of thunder.
My little room will suit you to a wonder,
And in that outer place alone I'll sleep,
And watch and guard upon your women keep.

"And in this room between, that here you see,
Shall all your women sleep both well and soft,
And snug within, yourself alone shall be.
And if you sleep well, come back soon and oft,
No matter what the weather be aloft!
Just one last drink! And when you feel inclined,
Now all of you know just where your bed to find!"

The night cup to the company was passed,
And all the curtains then were closely drawn,
And so it was not long until the last
Of all the folk from out the room had gone.
But still the pelting rain kept on and on,
And such a storm of wind blew all around,
You could not hear a single other sound.

Fair Cressida was to her chamber brought,
Together with a personal maid or two,
And Pandar, doing all a good host ought,
With many a bow, to her then said adieu,
But added, "At this door not far from you,
Your women will be lodged across the hall,
And if you want them, you need only call."

So Cressida was safely tucked in bed,
And all disposed of, just as Pandar planned,
And I have carefully explained and said;
If any then would tramp about, or stand
And talk, the rest did scold and all demand
That those who made the racket should keep still
And let the others sleep who had the will.

NOW Pandar knew the game he had to play,
And how to manage every point therein,
And all in a preliminary way
Now being well, was ready to begin;
And first the little door he doth unpin,
And entering there as still as any stone,
By Troilus he sat him down alone.

And then he had a story to relate
Of all these things, from very start to end.
"Get ready," said he, "heaven's joys await
On thee, if thou wilt but attend!"
"Saint Venus," Troilus replied, "now send
Thy aid, for never have I had such need,
Nor ever felt such fright for any deed!"

Said Pandar, "Don't be in the least afraid,
For all shall turn out just as you desire;
Tonight I say your fortune shall be made,
Or else tonight the fat be in the fire."
"O blessed Venus, now my heart inspire,"
Cried Troilus, "and in thy service high
My time forever I shall occupy!

"And if there reigned, O Venus, queen of mirth,
Aspects of Saturn, or of Mars malign,
Or thou wert quenched or hindered at my birth,
Thy father pray that he this harm of mine
Will turn aside, and grant me joy divine,
For love of him for whom thou felt'st love's pain,
Adonis, by the fateful wild boar slain!

"O Jove, thou lover of Europa fair,
Who as a bull didst carry her away,
Now help! O Mars, who bloody cloak dost bear,
For love of Venus, hinder me not I pray!

O Phoebus, think how Daphne pined one day
Beneath the bark, and to a laurel grew,
And help me now, for love of her so true!

"O Mercury, I beg in Herse's name,
Though Pallas was against Aglauros set,
Now help! Diana, let not modest shame
Dissuade thee now to aid me and abet!
O Fatal Sisters, ere my nurse made yet
My swaddling clothes, my destiny ye spun,
So help me in this work that is begun!"

SAID Pandar, "O, you chicken-hearted wretch!
Are you afraid because you think she'll bite?
Put something on—this over-cloak just fetch
Along, and follow me to see a sight!
But wait, I'll go ahead, to make all right!"
Then he undid a little secret door,
And Troilus waiting, he went on before.

The wind so roared and rumbled round about,
No other sound could anywhere be heard,
And those whose beds stood near the door without,
They slept and not a single person stirred,
For none had caught a whisper or a word.
Then Pandar found the door, without a light,
Where they all lay, and softly shut it tight.

He came again, quite still and stealthily,
But Cressida awoke and cried, "Who's there?"
"Dear niece," he softly said, "it's only me!
I hope I haven't given you a scare!"
And whispering low, he begged her to beware;
"No word," he said, "that curious folk can hear!
We don't want meddlers now to interfere!"

"How in the world," she asked, "did you get here,
And they not know a thing about it all?"
"At this trap-door," he answered, drawing near.
"Perhaps," said Cressida, "I'd better call."
"What, God forbid!" he answered still and small.
"If we by anyone should thus be caught,
They might think what they never would have thought.

"Like sleeping dogs, you know—just let them sleep!
Don't ever give a chance for vague surmise.
Your women are in slumber sunk so deep,
You might pull down the town before their eyes,
And will sleep so until the sun shall rise;
And when I've told you what I have to say,
As silent as I came, I'll go away.

"Dear niece, I'm sure you quite well understand,
And all, I think, agree in this," he said,
"That if you have a certain man in hand,
Whose hopes with honeyed words you long have fed,
And yet you set a fool's cap on his head,
I mean, with someone else you are too thick,—
Why, that's a shameful and a nasty trick.

"Now let me tell why I say this to you.
You know yourself as well as any wight,
That all your love is promised and is due
To Troilus, that good and noble knight,
And with such pledges you your faith did plight,
You never would your love to him deny,
Unless, indeed, the fault in him should lie.

"But here's the point, that since to bed I went,
This Troilus, with something on his brain,
Has by a gutter, through a secret vent,
Into my chamber come in all this rain,
Of course unknown to all, let me explain,
Save me alone in all the town of Troy,
I swear as I have hope of heaven's joy.

"Now he has come this night in such great grief
That I'm afraid lest he may lose his mind,
For he is hurt and wild beyond belief,
And now the reason for all this I find,
His faith in you a friend has undermined,
Who says you love a fellow named Horast,
For grief of which this night may be his last."

CRESSIDA heard this tale with great surprise,
And therewithal she felt her heart grow cold,
And suddenly exclaimed, with tears and sighs,

"Alas, I thought, whatever tales were told,
My sweetheart would not me so lightly hold
For false! Alas, they'll drive me to my death,
These liars with their foul and poisoned breath!

"Horast! And me be false to Troilus!
Indeed I never knew him," answered she.
"Alas, what wicked spirit told him thus!
But Troilus tomorrow I shall see,
And from these charges I myself shall free,
In his and in the eyes of all good men,"
And thereupon she sighed and sighed again.

"O God," she cried, "these blessings temporal,
Which scholars falsely call felicity,
With bitterness are mingled and with gall!
God only knows what anguish then hath he
Who sees his empty joys before him flee!
For either joys arrive inopportune,
Or else they flit and vanish all too soon!

"O fickle fate! O worldly joy unstable!
Of men thou makest but a sport and play!
All know that they to hold their joy are able,
Or know it not—there is no other way.
Now if one knows it not, how may he say
That he of perfect joy perceives the spark,
If ignorance still leaves him in the dark?

"But if he knows that joy is transitory,
Since joy in every worldly thing must flee,
This troubling thought diminishes the glory
Of earthly joy, and so in such degree,
Imperfect must be his felicity;
If loss of joy he fears a jot or tittle,
This proves that earthly joy is worth but little.

"And so this problem I must thus decide,
That verily, for aught that I can see,
No perfect joy can in this world abide.
But O, thou viper, wicked jealousy!
O folly, faithless, envious of me!
Why has thou bred in Troilus distrust,
And I in all things ever true and just!"

"You know," said Pandar, "that of Troilus"—
"Why, uncle dear," she cried, "who told him so?
Alas, why does my sweetheart treat me thus?"
"O, well," he said, "the way of the world, you know.
But what's gone wrong, we'll make the right way go.
The way to stop all this with you doth rest,
And everything will turn out for the best."

"So shall I do tomorrow," answered she,
"And in a way I'm sure will satisfy."
"Tomorrow?" he cried, "as well eternity!
No, no, we cannot let this thing slip by!
Old clerks have written in their wisdom high
That peril with delaying, strikes within.
No, such delayings are not worth a pin!

"There comes a fitting time for everything,
And when a room's afire or a hall,
It's better folk at once some help should bring,
Than stand and argufy amongst them all,
'How chanced this candle in the straw to fall?'
The harm is done the while they thus debate,
To lock the stable door is then too late.

"And niece, one thing I hope you'll let me say,
If all the night you leave him in this state,
Your love for him has been but vain display.
That's how it seems to me at any rate.
You can't abandon him to such a fate,
You know yourself, 'twould be the height of folly
To leave him in this dangerous melancholy."

"My love a vain display! You never loved
As I have loved," indignantly she cried.
"Well, that," he said, "remains yet to be proved!
But since by me you think you're justified,
I wouldn't let him in this sorrow bide,
I swear by Jove who in Olympus reigns,
No, not for all the gold that Troy contains!

"Now, look, if you who are his only love,
Shall put his life all night in jeopardy,
Just for a trifle, by the God above,
Both inconsiderate this act would be

And show in you a bad propensity.
If you abandon him, I'm frank to say,
Nor wisdom nor yet kindness you display."

"At least," said Cressida, "this can I do,
And that will bring him some relief and ease.
Convey to him this ring with stone of blue,
For there is nothing will him better please,
Except myself, or more his wrath appease,
And say to my sweetheart that all his sorrow
Is without ground, as he shall see tomorrow."

"O pshaw," said he, "a fig for all your ring!
The sort of ring he needs must have a stone
With power enough the dead to life to bring,
And such a ring, dear niece, you do not own.
Discretion from your head seems to have flown!
O time, O wasted opportunity,
O cursed sloth, O heedless sluggardy!

"Do you not know that men of courage high,
Feel strongly and are quick and sharp in action?
A fool in jealous rage one might pass by,
For shallow minds are shallow in distraction;
A few fair words will give them satisfaction,
They'll wait until you're ready to be kind,
But this is quite another thing, you'll find.

"This man is of such high and gentle heart,
His sorrows with his death he well may wreak;
Be sure, however sorely he may smart,
No jealous word to you he'll ever speak.
And now no further subterfuges seek,
Insist no longer on your wilful pride,
But say the word his heart to cheer and guide.

"I've told you now the peril he is in,
And not a soul of him has caught a sight.
Besides there need be neither harm nor sin,
For I shall be at hand through all the night.
You know he never will transgress his right,
And as your knight, you must in him confide.
I'll fetch him here as soon as you decide."

NOW so distressing was all this to hear,
And seemed, besides, so likely on its face,
And Troilus, her knight, to her so dear,
So secret, too, his coming and the place,
That though there was a risk of some disgrace,
Considering everything, just how it stood,
No wonder if she took it all for good.

"God knows," said Cressida, "it makes me sad
To hear of my dear love's distress and woe;
To help him in his sorrow I'd be glad,
If what was best to do I could but know;
But whether you should stay or for him go,
I am, till heaven some direction send,
But at Dulcarnon, at my wits' last end."

"Dulcarnon?" said he, "let me tell you, dear,
That means, 'last hope of those of feeble mind.'
Such persons in their heads are never clear,
But stay for very sloth perversely blind,
And for such folk this saying is designed;
But you are wise, and what we have in hand,
Calls for no subtle wit to understand."

"Well, uncle," said she, "do as you think best!
But let me first, before he comes, arise.
And since my trust in you two all doth rest,
And since you both are most discreet and wise,
I beg you will this matter so devise,
My honor and his wish to satisfy,
For everything in your hands now doth lie."

"Well spoken that," he said, "my niece so dear!
You've shown you have a wise and gentle heart!
But just lie still and let him come right here,
Your messages you can as well impart,
And may you ease each other's pain and smart.
And now at last, O Venus, praise to thee,
For soon some happy times we here shall see."

TROILUS now beside his lady kneeling,
Full soberly beside his lady's bed,
Extends to her his greetings with such feeling,

She waxes all at once a rosy red;
She could not speak a word, to save her head,
On seeing him so sudden and unbidden,
Come from the place in which he had been hidden.

But Pandar always knew just what to do,
And now to break the ice, his jokes began,
And said, "See how this lord doth kneel to you!
Just rest your eyes upon this gentleman!"
And quickly then, he for a cushion ran,
And said, "Take this, and on it kneel your fill!
And may your hearts be purged of every ill!"

Just why did she not order him to rise,—
If sorrow drove the thought out of her mind,
I cannot say, or kneeling in this wise
She thought as manners only was designed,
But this I know, she was in so far kind,
That though she sighed, nevertheless she kissed him
And to a seat beside her did assist him.

"All's ready now," said Pandar, "to begin!
That's right, dear niece, these curtains interfere,
Just let him sit upon your bed within;
It's easier so each other's words to hear."
Then he withdrew and left the way all clear,
And took a light and sat down by the fire,
As though to read he felt a great desire.

And Cressida, assured that all was right,
And that she stood on safe and solid ground,
Yet thinking as her servant and her knight
No lack of faith in her he should have found,
Now felt herself constrained in duty bound,
Though faithful love had caused this thing to be,
To speak to him about his jealousy.

"Though love," she said, "should be of such a kind,
That no true lover ever ought or may
Encourage opposition in his mind,
Yet still, because I've seen in every way
Your faithfulness and service day by day,
And that your heart was mine has been so plain,
This led me to have pity on your pain.

"And since I've ever found you good and wise,
For which, my precious heart and my true knight,
I thank you now as far as in me lies,
Though not as much, perhaps, as were your right,
Yet still according to my wit and might,
Whatever grief hereafter may befall,
My heart is yours and shall be all in all.

"And that, I'm sure, you do and will believe.
To say this, sweetheart, goes against the grain,
But you must not threat too deeply grieve,
Although I seem upon you to complain;
For in the end this present grief and pain
That holds your heart and mine in heaviness,
I shall remove and every harm redress.

"But precious one, I know not how nor why
That viper jealousy, insidious thief,
Should thus into your bosom creep so sly,
The which to both of us is cause of grief.
Alas, that thou shouldst thus beyond belief
Exalt low jealousy to such a place!
May Jove such thoughts from out your heart erase!

"But O, thou Jove, from whom all things have life,
Is this an honor to thy deity,
That guiltless folk should suffer here in strife
And yet the guilty one all free goes he?
O, were it lawful to complain on thee,
This charge I'd bring against thy mighty name
Of causeless jealousy I bear the blame.

"Another shame is this, that folk abuse
True love and say, 'Yea, jealousy is love!'
A bushel of venom such folk will excuse
If but a grain of love therein they shove.
But God knows this, who lives and reigns above,
If it be liker love or liker hate,
And by its name we should it designate.

"Some sorts of jealousy, I will confess,
Are more excusable than other kinds,
As when there's cause, or when folk long repress
Some harsh fantastic notion in their minds,

Which in expression no free outlet finds,
And on itself it thus doth grow and feed;
For such repression is a gentle deed.

"And some are filled with fury and despite
So full that it surpasses all restraint—
But, sweetheart, you are not in such plight,
Thank God, and all your grieving and your plaint,
I call it an illusive lover's taint
From love's excess, and from anxiety,
From which this long time you have not been free,

"At which I grieve, but do no anger feel.
But now, if this will set your heart at rest,
Just as you will, by oath or by ordeal,
By lot, or any way you think the best,
I'm ready here to undergo the test.
If I am guilty, take my life away!
What more, alas, is there that I can say?"

Some tears with that, like shining drops of dew,
Fell from her eyes, but only two or three,
"Thou knowest, God, that Cressida untrue
To Troilus is not, nor e'er shall be!"
And then upon her couch she laid her head,
And sighing sore, covered it with the sheet,
And held her peace in silence quite complete.

MAY heaven bring relief for all this sorrow!
There's ground for hope, for such is heaven's way;
For I have seen on many a misty morrow
Following oft a merry summer's day,
And after winter, comes along the May.
'Tis known, and vouched for by authorities,
That storms are presages of victories.

Poor Troilus, when he heard how she spoke,
Imagine how her chiding words struck deep!
A heavy stick it was that struck this stroke,
To hear and see his lady-love thus weep;
The cramp of death he felt upon him creep,
And every tear he saw his lady shed,
Strangled his heart till it lay cold and dead.

And mentally the hour he did curse
That he came there, or that when he was born!
For what was bad, was now turned into worse,
And for love's labors lost, he could but mourn,
And count him of all creatures most forlorn.
O Pandar, thought he, all thy cunning guile,
Has come to naught but this, alack the while!

At these sad thoughts he humbly hung his head,
And fell upon his knees and deeply sighed.
What could he say? All life from him had fled,
Her chiding words his grief so magnified,
But when he could, at last he thus replied:
"When all is known, I swear in heaven's name,
Then you will see that I am not to blame."

Though sorrow at his heart so sternly pressed,
There fell not from his eye a single tear,
His inmost nature was so strained and stressed
No movement of his spirit could appear;
Sensation now of sorrow or of fear
Or aught beside, all fled was out of town,
And in a swoon he suddenly fell down.

O, what a dreadful thing this was to see!
How still he lay, but Pandar got up fast,
"Hush, niece! Keep still or we are lost!" said he;
"Don't be afraid!" and took him at the last,
And tearing off his clothes, he quickly cast
Him in her bed. "O Cressida," he cried,
"Have you a human heart in your inside!

"Dear niece, unless you try to help us now,
Your Troilus is ever lost and lorn."
"That would I gladly do if I knew how,"
She cried. "Alas that I was ever born!"
"There's naught to do except pull out the thorn
That sticketh in his heart," wise Pandar said.
"Say 'All's forgiven,' and raise him from the dead."

"That were to me," she said, "a thing more dear
Than all the gold the circling sun goes round."
And thereupon she swore him in his ear,

"By all the oaths by which I can be bound,
I am not angry,"—yet he made no sound.
"It's Cressida, O speak, my precious heart!"
But from his trance she could not make him start.

His wrists and palms they then began to chafe,
With water both his temples they did lave,
From out his bitter bonds to bring him safe,
And many a loving kiss to him she gave,
To call him from this lethargy so grave,
Until a breath he drew, and none too soon,
And so began to come out of his swoon.

And when some notice he began to take,
Full sore he was abashed and mortified,
And with a sigh, when he was quite awake,
"Where am I?" first with feeble voice he cried.
"What trouble for you all I've made," he sighed.
"O Troilus, now be a man!" said she.
"Why do you act like this? For shame on thee!"

Her arm around his neck she gently laid,
Forgiving him with many a soft embrace,
And his apologies he humbly made,
In manner fitting to the time and place.
These she received at once with right good grace,
And spoke to him so kindly and so well,
Her loving words his sorrow soon dispel.

"This candle and I, so far as I can spy,"
Said Pandar, "are no longer here required!
The light is harmful to a sick man's eye!
But now you have the chance so long desired,
Before the fleeting time shall be expired,
Let joy alone with your hearts abide,"—
And took his candle to the chimney-side.

AT LAST this lady's mind was set and clear!
Since he all oaths she could or would devise
Had sworn to her and banished all her fear,
She saw no reason now to bid him rise.
Yet less than oaths quite often satisfies
In such a case as this, for every man
Who loveth well, will do the best he can.

At first she asked, insisting she would know,
What man, and where, and also why,
He jealous was, and no cause to be so,
And also all the signs he judged her by
She bade him tell and not a thing deny,
Or else, she said, she saw no other way,
She'd have to think a trick he tried to play.

And when he saw she would not be denied,
Or if she were, her doubts would be increased,
Choosing the lesser evil, he replied,
"It was," he said, "at such and such a feast"—
And thought she might have looked at him at least—
O, I don't know, he said some thing or other,
'Twas all as well, one answer or another.

"My dearest heart," she said, "though it were true,
Why such an imputation must you draw?
For by the God above who made us two,
No harm in that I ever meant or saw!
Your vain suspicions are not worth a straw!
Such childish reasons scarce deserve the thanking,
You really ought to have a right good spanking!"

Then Troilus began again to sigh,
And new fears at his heart began to twine.
"Alas," he said, "my errors heavy lie
Upon my conscience, precious sweetheart mine,
But now all foolish thoughts I will resign,
And shall hereafter not again offend.
Do what you will—I'm yours unto the end!"

"True mercy," said she, "is not slow or strained,
Forgiven and forgotten be the past!
But let this night in mind be long retained;
Of jealous doubts, let this one be the last!"
"O yes, dear heart!" he promised quick and fast.
"And now," she said, "the pain I've given thee,
Sweetheart, I beg that you forgive it me!"

TROILUS felt such glad relief at this,
With trust in God and in his lady's grace,
And courage drawn from his so sudden bliss,
He seized and held her in a close embrace.

And Pandar, feeling somewhat out of place,
Lay down to sleep and said, "If you are wise,
Don't swoon again, or others may arise!"

The helpless lark, what can it do or say
After the hawk hath caught it in his claw?
Not otherwise it was with her that day;
Like it or not, this is all nature's law.
And though my tale throughout a year I draw,
Lo, I, as does my author, still must tell,
After their grief, their time of joy as well.

Cressida in his arms thus boldly taken,
As all wise clerks have said in books of old,
Shook like an aspen leaf by breezes shaken,
As his strong arms about her body fold;
And Troilus, all freed of care so cold,
Gave thanks to those bright Gods, glorious seven—
In sundry ways thus folk are brought to heaven.

Troilus in arms his love doth hold and strain,
And whispers, "Precious heart, now you are caught!
In all the world there liveth but we twain!
Now you must yield, evasion helpeth naught!"
But of evasion she had little thought;
"Had I not yielded," said she, "sweetheart dear,
Before the night, I would not now be here!"

O TRUE it is, before they can be cured,
Whether of fever or other great disease,
The sick must drink, for all they have endured,
Full bitter drink, and for their better ease,
Must oft partake of things that do not please.
All this to Troilus may be applied,
Who after pain is glad and satisfied.

And sweetness now seemed more than ever sweet,
For all the bitterness that went before;
And now the time goes by on winged feet,
In joy so great, it never could be more,
Or better pay for all the griefs they bore.
And here I beg that lovers all will heed
This good example at their time of need!

And Cressida, from fear and dread all free,
With faith and trust in him now absolute,
Made him such feast that it was good to see
Such faithful service bear such happy fruit.
And as the woodbine, growing near its root,
Doth clasp the tree with tendrils intertwined,
So they their arms about each other wind.

And like the hushed expectant nightingale,
Who ceases after she begins to sing
If sound of voices loud her ears assail,
Or in the hedges stirreth anything,
But then thereafter lets her song out-ring,
So Cressida, released from all her fear,
Opened her heart for him to look and hear.

And like the man who sees his death impending,
And die he must, for aught that he can tell,
Yet sudden rescue brings a happy ending,
And all the things he dreaded, turn out well,
So now to Troilus like fortune fell,
For now at last he hath his lady sweet—
God grant we may with no worse fortune meet!

Her slender arms, her back so straight and soft,
Her yielding sides, so long and smooth and bright,
He gently stroked, nor failed to note full oft
Her snowy throat, her rounding breasts so white,
Whereon he gazed in heavenly delight.
Such joy he felt he scarce knew what to do,
A thousand kisses seemed to him but few.

"O Love," exclaimeth he, "O Charity!
Thy mother also, Citherea sweet,
After thyself exalted may she be,
O Venus, gracious planet, I repeat,
And next to Venus, Hymen, I thee greet!
For never man was to you Gods more bound
Than I, who from my cares relief have found.

"O Love benign, thou holy bond of things,
All they who seek thy grace, but scorn thy aid,
Their love shall fly but feebly without wings.

By thy goodwill man's fortune must be made;
For faithful service ne'er so well displayed,
Were all for naught, this dare I well assert,
Did not thy gift surpass our poor desert.

"And since that I, who merited the least
To win thy gracious favor and support,
Have had my joys extended and increased
And am exalted in such lofty sort
That widest bounds to hold my joys fall short,
What can I do, but words of reverent praise
Unto thy bounty and thy goodness raise!"

HIS prayer he ended with a kiss or two,
Which part of it at least was well received,
And then he said, "I would to God I knew
How you of every grief might be relieved!
Was ever man," he said, "so little grieved
As I, on whom the fairest and the best
Deigneth her loving heart to bring to rest!

"Here one may see that mercy passeth right,
As my experience tells me feelingly,
Who am unworthy of you, lady bright;
But sweetheart mine, in your benignity,
Believe that all unworthy though I be,
Yet needs I must amend and still improve,
But through the lofty virtue of my love.

"One favor more, dear heart, I beg beside,
Since God hath wrought me but to do thy will,
Be thou my ever-present, helpful guide,
For thou hast power of good and power of ill.
So teach me, sweetheart mine, that I may still
Deserve thy thanks, and thy good counsel lend
To save me from all acts that may offend.

"For truly, fairest of all womankind,
This dare I say, that truth and diligence
Through all my life thou shalt within me find;
And if I sin with injury prepense,
Present or absent, I shall waive defence,
And yield myself to thee at that same hour,
As humbly subject to thy womanly power."

"Enough," she cried, "O thou my richest treasure,
My ground of ease, and all I hold most dear,
I trust in thee beyond all bound and measure!
But let us talk no more of future fear,
There needs no more than thou hast promised here.
I am content, befall what may befall;
Welcome, my knight, my peace, my all in all!"

TO TELL the limits of their great delight
For me were sheer impossibility,
But all can guess who such a festal night
Have ever known, I trust, in some degree;
And of these lovers twain, I merely say to thee,
That night twixt joy and fear they realize
How love may be a serious enterprise.

O night of love, by them so long time sought,
So happy now at last in consummation,
With my own soul I gladly would have bought
The lease division of its delectation!
Away now every check to inclination,
And let them in this bliss of heaven dwell,
Too great for mortal tongue to sing or tell.

But though I cannot tell you everything,
As might my author with his greater gift,
The burden of his song yet shall I sing,
And all his thought employ with proper thrift,
And if I've added to his general drift
In praise of love, I leave it in your hand,
Remove it from my tale or let it stand.

For all my words, in this and every part,
Are spoken under your correction all,
Who better know the secrets of the heart
Than I, and therefore I upon you call
To change or take away in general,
Such words as seem to you were best omitted;
But now to come back where our tale we quitted.

THESE two whom we have left in love's embrace,
Could not endure the thought of separation;
They scarce believed that they were in that place,
Or else were filled with fear and consternation

That all this night was but hallucination,
And oft they said, for doubt this was but seeming,
"O art thou there, or am I only dreaming?"

With such intentive look he on her gazed,
His eyes were fixed unmoving on her face;
"O sweetheart," he exclaimed, "the Gods be praised,
And is it true that thou art in this place?"
"Yes, sweetheart mine, and all by heaven's grace!"
She says, and therewithal a kiss bestows,
That where his spirit is, he scarcely knows.

And he neglected not to kiss her eyes,
And when he did, he said, "O eyes so clear,
In you the cause of all my sorrows lies,
Ye double weapons of my lady dear!
Though mercy seemeth to be written here,
The text, forsooth, is very hard to find.
How is it, without bonds thou couldst me bind?"

Within his arms his lady he doth take,
And full a thousand times he gently sighed,
Not sighs of sorrow, such as sad men make
From grief, or when by sickness they are tried,
But easy sighs, which showed how satisfied
He was, and how his love was deeply seated,
Such sighs he drew, and oft and oft repeated.

And then they spoke of many varied things,
As in this situation would arise,
And playfully they interchanged their rings,
But what the mottoes were, you may surmise;
A brooch of gold, as azure as the skies,
Set with a ruby heart, she gave him too,
And pinned it to his shirt as love pledge true.

Do you suppose that any grasping wretch,
Who chides at love and holds it in despite,
From all the profit he from gold can fetch,
Was ever so enriched with pure delight
As these two knew, in measure infinite?
Nay, they can never know, so God me save,
Such perfect joy who niggardly behave.

And if they say they do, they merely lie,
Those busy wretches, full of woe and dread;
They call love madness and against it cry,
But ever they in grief shall make their bed,
Nor yet have joy of money, white nor red!
So let them live in grief and in mischance,
But lovers' joys may heaven still enhance.

Would God that all those wretches who despise
The gentle works of love had ears as long
As Midas had, that king so penny-wise;
Or might be served with drink as hot and strong
As Crassus drank, for deeds so harsh and wrong;
For greed is vice, as all old stories show,
And love is virtue, let who will say no.

THESE happy two, whose joys I've been reporting,
Who now at last in love were so secure,
They fell to talking, and in playful sporting
They told how, when and where they first were sure
They knew each other, and how they did endure
The griefs now passed; for all that might annoy
This night was turned at last to perfect joy!

If in their talk of joy they came abrupt
On any woe of times now past and gone,
With kisses all their tale they interrupt,
And thus again to joy are brought anon.
One thing alone their hearts were set upon,
To free their joy from all its base alloys,
And former grief with joy to counterpoise.

You'll scarce expect that I should speak of sleep,
The topic seems, indeed, not pertinent.
A night of vigil they were glad to keep,
And lest this time, that so much to them meant,
Should slip away before they could prevent,
The happy hours were fully occupied
With all the gentle arts to love allied.

THE cock, astrologer in his own way,
Began to beat his breast and then to crow,
And Lucifer, the messenger of day,

Began to rise and forth her beams to throw,
And eastward rose, as you perhaps may know,
Fortuna Major—for the night was fled,
And Cressida to Troilus thus said:

"Life of my heart, my trust and my delight,
That I was born, alas, to such a woe!
For we must part with parting of the night.
'Tis time that thou must rise and hence must go,
Or I am lost, and ever shall be so!
O night, why wilt thou not above us hover,
As long as when Jove was Alcmena's lover?

"O night so black, as onc in old books reads,
Thou wert designed by God this world to hide
At certain seasons with thy inky weeds,
That men might then in rest and peace abide;
Yet beasts may well lament and men may chide,
That though by toil through all the day distressed,
Away thou flee'st and grantest them no rest!

"Thou dost, alas, thy time too quickly waste,
O heedless night! The maker of mankind
Curse thee for thy unnecessary haste,
And to our hemisphere so firm thee bind,
Thy way below thou ne'er again shalt find!
For through thy heedless hieing out of Troy
Thus have we hastily foregone our joy!"

TROILUS, too, at these sad bodings felt
The weight of heavy sorrow on him press;
His heart began in bloody tears to melt,
For never yet such grievous heaviness
He e'er had known or woe so comfortless;
And Cressida, his lady, he did take
Within his arms and in this manner spake:

"O cruel day, denouncer of the joy
That night and love have stolen and concealed,
Accursed be thy coming into Troy,
For all to thy bright eyes is now revealed!
Envious day, what will thy spying yield?
What hast thou lost, and hunt for in this place?
May God put out thy light in dark disgrace!

"Alas, with wrong thou chargest love of guilt,
Thou hateful day! May thine be all the pain of hell!
For many a lover hast thou slain, and wilt
Yet slay, for light grants them no place to dwell!
Why must thou proffer here thy light to sell?
Go sell to them who tiny seals engrave!
We want thee not, we need no daylight save!"

Titan, the sun, in like words did he chide,
And said, "O fool, well may men thee despise,
Thou hast all night fair Daybreak at thy side,
And yet permittest her so soon to rise
And so distress all lovers in this wise!
What, stay in bed, thou Titan, with thy Morrow!
May heaven grant the both of you have sorrow!"

He sighed and said, for yet he was not done,
"My lady true, and of my weal and woe
The very root, thou fair and goodly one,
Must I arise? Alas, and must I so?
My heart is cleft in twain that I must go!
Since all the joy I have abides with you,
With my poor life what then is left to do?

"What hope is left? In truth I know not how
Or when, alas, I may occasion see
To be again with thee as I am now!
God knows, 'twill be a heavy weird to dree!
And if desire now so tortures me,
I seem but dead till to thy arms I turn,
How shall I longer time from thee sojourn?

"But nevertheless, my precious lady bright,
If I were sure beyond the slightest doubt,
That I, your servant and your faithful knight,
Within your heart were compassed round about
As you in mine, so naught can shut me out,
The world for me could hold no greater gain,
And that good thought would lighten all my pain."

TO THIS fair Cressida replied anon,
And sighing said, "Beloved sweetheart dear,
The game in very truth is so far gone
That Phoebus first shall fall from out his sphere,

And doves and eagles as true friends appear,
And every rock from out its station start,
Ere Troilus from Cressida's poor heart!

"Love doth thee in my heart so deep engrave,
That though I would expel thee from my thought,
As heaven's grace my weary soul shall save,
Though I should die, I could accomplish naught!
And for the love of him who hath us wrought,
Let no such fancy creep within your brain,
To cause me thus to perish with the pain.

"If you hold me as firmly in your mind
As I hold you, I'll be content and glad,
And if it turns out so, then I shall find
No further happiness for heaven to add!
But, love, let's talk no more of glad and sad,
Be true to me, there's nothing more to say,
For I am thine, forever and a day!

"Be thus content, and cast away all fear!
Thou hast what ne'er shall have another man.
And if it be thy will, O sweetheart dear,
Come back again as soon as e'er you can,
Thy pleasure here shall be no greater than
My own, so may I hope for heaven's bliss!—"
And took him in her arms with many a kiss.

SO WILLY-NILLY, since the day was near,
Troilus got up and dressed beside the bed,
And in his arms he took his lady dear,
A hundred times, ere on his way he sped,
And with a voice as though at heart he bled,
He cried aloud, "Farewell, my precious sweeting!
God grant us soon a safe and happy meeting!"

To this no word for sorrow she replied,
And grief that thus they must be rent in twain;
And Troilus unto the palace hied,
As woe-begone as she, I dare maintain.
So heavy was the burden of the pain
Of joys remembered, but so sudden vanished,
He felt as one from heaven sternly banished.

He reached the palace as the daylight grew,
And softly to his bed he planned to slink
And sleep as late as he was wont to do—
But planned in vain, for not a single wink
Of sleep into his heart might gently sink,
For pondering she who now his life controlled
Was better than he guessed a thousandfold.

About his loving thoughts now twist and wind
Her every word and every loving glance,
Impressing clear and firm upon his mind
Each slightest point and circumstance;
And at the memory of his happy chance,
Love bursts anew in flames of high desire,
Though little feels he now the burning fire.

Cressida, also, in the selfsame wise
The worth, the gaiety, and every deed
Of Troilus recalled before her eyes,
And all remembrances for him so plead,
That from this love she never can be freed;
She longs again to have him in such plight
That she alone may bring to him delight.

NOW Pandar, seeing day was there at last,
Came to his niece, and fairly doth her greet.
"All night," he said, "it rained so hard and fast,
That I am dreadfully afraid, my sweet,
Your dreams will not be pleasant to repeat.
All night the rain kept me quite wide awake,
I greatly fear it's made our heads all ache."

Then he drew near and said, "How do you do
This sunny morn? How do you feel today?"
Cressida answered, "None the better for you,
Fox that you are! The Lord will you repay!
For you have managed things in your own way,
I now can see, for all your words so fair!
You fooled me well with your deceptive air!"

Cressida strove her blushing face to hide
Behind the sheet, and grew for shame all red.
But Pandar underneath the bedclothes pried,

"Dear Cressida, if I must die," he said,
"Have here a sword and smite off my poor head!"
He thrust his arm beneath her neck to twist
The covers off, and then his niece he kissed.

No need to tell how they were reconciled!
If God forgave his death, then should not she
Forgive her uncle? Thus the time they whiled
Away in great amicability,
As good friends now as anyone could be,
Till in good time to her own house she went
And left her uncle very well content.

TO TROILUS let us now turn again,
Who long abed in wakeful tossing lay;
For Pandar soon he sent some of his men
To bid him hasten thither right away,
And Pandar came without a no or nay,
And greeting him in manner dignified,
Upon his bed he sat down at his side.

And Troilus, moved by the deep affection
Which for his friend within his heart now lies,
Falls on his knees in absolute subjection,
Nor from that humble place he will arise,
But thank with grateful thank he multiplies,
A thousand times, and oft the day doth bless
His friend was born to save him from distress.

"O friend," he said, "of friends the very best
That ever was or ever was heard tell,
Thou hast in heaven brought my soul to rest
From Phlegethon, the fiery flood of hell;
A thousand times a day if I should sell
Myself to serve and honor only thee,
Enough reward and pay it would not be.

"The sun which moves above in all man's sight,
Saw never yet, this dare I will aver,
A fairer than my dearest lady bright,
And to my death I shall be bound to her;
The thanks for all this favor I refer
To Love, who honors me with kind assistance,
And also, Pandar, to thy wise persistence.

"What thou hast given is no little thing,
And I shall pay thee thanks forever and aye!
And why? Because thy faithful help did bring
Me back to life, who else were dead this day"—
And then upon his bed again he lay.
Soberly Pandar listened at his side
Till he was through, and thus replied:

"My dearest friend, if aught I've done for thee,
God knows it is to me a great relief,
And I'm as glad of it as you can be.
But now take heed that we come not to grief,
For there is danger still of this mischief,
That now that thou art settled in thy bliss,
Thyself may cause affairs to go amiss.

"Of fickle fortune's sharp adversities,
The very worst misfortune of them all,
Is this, to know and lose all joy and ease,
And have but bitter memories to recall.
Exert thy wisdom such fate to forestall;
Be not too rash, nor of thyself too sure,
Or harm will quickly come and long endure.

"Thou art at ease, and hold thee well therein,
For just as true that red is every fire,
To keep demands as much skill as to win.
Then bridle well thy speech and thy desire,
For worldly joys hang by a subtle wire,
And for sad proof, it breaketh quick and oft,
Wherefore the need to walk both light and soft."

"I hope," said Troilus, "before men's eyes,
Dear friend, that I such heed shall take,
That through my fault no danger shall arise,
And rashness I abjure for her dear sake.
You need not fear my promise I shall break,
If you but knew the secrets of my mind,
Then mighty little cause for fear you'd find."

And then he told him of his happy night,
And how at first he was afraid, and why,
And said, "I swear upon my honor bright
And by my faith in you and God on high,

I never knew what loving did imply;
For as my heart's desires rose in height,
The greater grew my love and my delight.

"To me myself it is a mystery,
For now I feel in me a nature new,
A thing that makes a different man of me."
And Pandar said, "Yes, I suppose it's true,
That he who once in heaven's bliss may be,
He feels it all in quite another way
Than when he knew it by hear-say."

But now enough—though Troilus indeed
To speak of this doth never stop or tire,
And still to praise his lady would proceed,
Exalting all her bounty higher and higher,
And thanking Pandar all he could require,
Then in again bran-new he ever starts,
Until his friend at night homeward departs.

SOON after this, by great good luck, it fell
He had a chance his night-watch to repeat,
For Pandar came the happy news to tell,
That Cressida, his lady, he should meet.
How then his heart with sudden joy doth beat!
His thanks to all the gods he then did pay,
And you can guess if he was glad and gay!

The manner of this meeting was again
Somewhat as I have told and as you know,
And so I shall not bother to explain,
But to the end now let us straightway go;
For Pandar still his faithful aid did show
And brought them to the place they liked the best,
And there they are in quiet and in rest.

You have no need, now they again are met,
To ask of me if they were happy there.
For what was good before, grows better yet
A thousandfold, with goodness still to spare.
And now they know no sorrow or no care,
For joy as great to them the kind gods send
As any human heart may comprehend.

This is no trifling thing that now I say,
'Tis something no man's wit can all comprise;
For each to other's will doth so obey
That all the joys that ancient clerks so wise
Have praised, counted as nothing in their eyes;
Their joy may not be written down in ink,
For it surpasses all that heart may think!

But cruel day, alack the fateful hour,
Again returns, as they by signs well knew,
And they must yield to sorrow's greater power.
Full sad they were, full sad and pale of hue,
Reviling day with scornings ever new,
Calling it traitor, envious and worse—
O, bitterly the light of day they curse!

"Alas," said Troilus, "now it is plain
That Pyroeis and his team-mates three,
Which draw the bright sun's chariot in their train,
Have gone some short cut in despite of me,
And that is why the night so soon doth flee;
And if the sun will hasten thus the day,
No offerings on his altar shall I lay."

But day must come, and they must separate,
And after all was said that could be said,
They finally submit to their sad fate,
Yet for a meeting set a time ahead;
And thus for many a night their lives they led
As Fortune gave to them this ample joy,
To Cressida and Troilus of Troy.

IN GREAT content, in sport and merry songs,
Troilus passes now his happy days.
He spends, he jousts, his feastings he prolongs,
Himself in gaudy garments he arrays,
He has a world of folk about always,
The freshest and the best that he can find,
As suiting one of his so noble kind.

Such name and fame of him now circulate
Throughout the world, his honor and largess,
It mounts and rings at heaven's very gate;

And through his love he knows so great gladness
That in his heart he ever doth profess,
No lover in the world is more at ease
Or hath a love with greater power to please.

Though other ladies were both fair and kind,
Yet all the virtues in their natures set
About his heart one knot could not unbind
Of Cressida's so subtly woven net.
Enmeshed he was, and never shall he get
His freedom, nor a single part of it,
For no man's skill this net can e'er unknit.

And Pandar by the hand he oft would take,
And in the garden find a quiet place,
And such a glorious anthem there they'd make
Of Cressida and all her woman's grace,
And of the beauty of her form and face,
It was a heavenly joy his praise to hear,
And thus he sang unto his lady dear:

"O LOVE, that dost the earth and sea control,
O Love, that dost command the heavens high,
O Love, of blessed harmony the soul,
All nations rest beneath thy guiding eye!
Thou with whose law societies comply,
Thou in whose virtue loving couples dwell,
O Love, bind this accord of which I tell!

"The world that stands so firm on its foundation,
With all its many harmonies diverse;
The elements with all their contentation,
Yet held in bonds that nothing can disperse;
Phoebus that doth the earth in light immerse;
The moon that hath the lordship over night—
All these depend on Love and on his might.

"The sea that never falters in its flowing,
Restrains its floods to such a certain end,
However fiercely tempests may be blowing,
To drown the earth it never can ascend;
If aught the bridle from Love's hand should rend,
All harmonies at once would burst asunder,
And scatter all that Love now holdeth under.

"God grant, the author of all natural kind,
That with the bond of Love he will consent
In circling love all hearts so firm to bind,
Escape therefrom no man shall e'er invent;
And loveless hearts, let them by Love be bent
To learn to love, and thus in pity grow,
But faithful hearts may Love keep ever so!"

IN ALL events that at the siege occurred,
Troilus was ready now for fray or fight.
He was, indeed, unless the books have erred,
Save Hector, Troy's most celebrated knight,
And this increase of valor and of might,
All came from love, his lady's thanks to win,
Which thus had changed his heart and soul within.

In times of truce, a-hawking he would ride,
Or hunt the boar or lion or the bear;
From smaller beasts he always turned aside.
And when he on his homeward way would fare,
Full oft his lady at her window there,
As fresh as falcon just freed of its hood,
Smiled salutations down from where she stood.

Now most of love and virtue was his speech,
And he despised all actions mean and low,
Nor failed to practice what some men but preach,
To honor those who first did honor show,
And comfort those in sorrow and in woe;
And when he heard that any man fared well
In love, such news he liked to hear and tell.

He held each man in estimation slight,
Unless he were engaged in love's emprise—
I mean the men who ought to be of right.
Love fancies he himself could well devise
And dress himself in such a dashing wise
That all the youth there in the city thought
That all was well, whate'er he said or wrought.

And though he was himself of royal race,
He treated no man with unkindly pride;
Benign he was to each in every place,
For which he won high praise on every side.

For love demanded by its native grace,
That he should shun all envy, pride and ire,
All avarice and other base desire.

O DAUGHTER to Dione, lady bright,
And Cupid, too, thy blind and winged son;
Ye sisters nine, who on Parnassus' height
Abide beside the fountain Helicon,
Thus far, with you to guide, my tale hath won!
And now since ye on other ways will wend,
Honor and praise be yours, world without end!

Your aid hath helped me in my song to tell
How Troilus to joy at last attained,
Though with his joy there was some grief as well,
Just as my author in his day explained.
My third book by your aid its end hath gained,
And Troilus we leave in peace and joy,
And Cressida, within the town of Troy.

BOOK IV—
CHARGE & COUNTERCHARGE

CHARGE & COUNTERCHARGE

TOO short a fleeting time, alas the while,
Great joy endures, and Fortune wills it so,
Who truest seems when most she will beguile,
And most allures when she will strike a blow,
And from her wheel some hapless victim throw;
For when some wretch slips down and disappears,
She laughs at him and comforts him with jeers.

From Troilus she now began to turn
Her face, and paid to him but little heed;
She made his lady her true lover spurn,
And on her wheel she set up Diomede;
At which, in truth, my heart begins to bleed,
And now my pen, with which I faltering write,
Trembles for fear of what I must endite.

How Cressida her Troilus forsook,
Or at the least, how she became unkind,
Henceforth must be the matter of my book,
As ancient records bring the tale to mind.
Alas, that ever they a cause should find
To speak her harm! but if the records lie,
Shame on the head of slanderers I cry!

Ye daughters of black night! Ye furies three,
Ye who lament in everlasting pain,
Megaera, Alecto and Tisiphone!
Thou cruel Mars, Quirinus' father, deign
To aid my fourth book to its end to gain
And tell how loss of love and loss of life
May be the final end of lovers' strife!

The Grecian hosts, as I before have told,
Still lay in siege about the Trojan wall;

151

And when within the Lion beams of gold
From Phoebus on the Lion's breast first fall,
Then Hector doth his barons to him call,
And plan to meet the Greeks in open fight,
And work such injury as there they might.

I do not know how long it was between
The day they made their plan and when they meant
To fight, but with their arms all bright and keen,
With spears in hand and great bows tautly bent,
Hector with many a worthy warrior went
Before the town, for battle ready set,
And on the field their foeman soon they met.

The whole long day with all spears sharply ground,
With arrows, darts, with swords and heavy maces,
They fiercely fight, and horse and man confound,
While axes dash out brains and cleave men's faces;
But at the last the Trojan host retraces
Its steps, faltering where their captains led,
And in defeat at night they homeward fled.

That day Antenor yielded in the fight,
And Polydamas nor yet Menestheus,
Xanthippus, Sarpedon or Polynestor might,
Polites nor the Trojan Sir Ripheus
Withstand the Greeks, still less Sir Phebuseus,
And all his like; the harm that day done Troy
The city's hopes did very near destroy.

Thereafter the Greeks a truce agreed to make,
As Priam asked, the purpose to debate
Of changing prisoners in a give and take,
And for the surplus, money payments great.
This news at once began to circulate
Among both Greeks and Trojans far and near,
And very soon it came to Calchas' ear.

Assured that all was true as it was told,
Into the Greek assembly Calchas pressed,
Where sat the Grecian lords so wise and old,
And took his rightful place among the rest,
And solemnly he made them this request,
That they would do him so much reverence
To stop their noise and give him audience.

"My lords, I was a Trojan in past days,"
He said, "as doubtless all of you know well,
And know that Calchas merits Grecian praise,
For I came here your troubles to dispel,
And all your future conquest to foretell;
For you shall surely burn the Trojan town,
And all its walls the Greeks shall batter down.

"And how at last the Greeks shall win this prize
And seize the town and conquest full achieve,
You've heard me often in detail previse;
All this you know, my lords, as I believe,
And how the Grecian fortunes to retrieve,
I came in my own person here from Troy,
On your behalf my knowledge to employ,

"Renouncing all my treasure, well content
If I could but contribute to your ease.
Thus all my goods I left with free consent,
My only thought, my lords, was you to please;
Nor grieve I now at loss of these,
Nor shall I much be troubled at the cost
If all my property in Troy is lost—

"Except a daughter, whom I left behind,
Sleeping at home the night I slipped away.
How could a father be so far unkind,
So hard of heart! Rather than let her stay,
Had I but dragged her forth in night array!
And so, my lords, except you heed my sorrow,
Methinks I ne'er shall see another morrow.

"And I so long, my lords, have held my peace,
Because I saw no way to bring her here;
But now or never must come her release,
And soon I hope to see my daughter dear!
To beg your aid before you I appear!
Have pity on an old man in distress,
For you are cause of all my heaviness.

"Trojans enough you have as captives caught,
With one of these, if so your will it be,
Redemption for my daughter may be bought.
I beg you in your generosity,

One of so many captives give to me!
Why should you such a little thing refuse,
Since all the town and folk are yours to choose?

"For here again I faithfully will swear,
Just as Apollo hath it to me told,
And as the stars above likewise declare,
And auspices and auguries of old,
I swear by all these signs so manifold,
That fire and flame on all the town shall spread,
And Troy shall turn to ashes, cold and dead.

"Phoebus on high, and watery Neptune, too,
Who gave its walls unto the Trojan town,
Are angry at the Trojan folk untrue,
And eager now to tear those same walls down;
Laomedon, who bore the royal crown,
Refused to pay to them their proper hire,
For which their city shall be burned with fire."

REHEARSING thus his tale, this old man gray
And feeble to the Greeks doth humbly speak,
With tears as salty as the ocean spray
Fast running down on either withered cheek.
So long he begs and earnestly doth seek,
That at the last, to stop his long lament,
To give to him Antenor they consent.

When thus the long debate was brought to close,
Calchas arrangements with the legates made
Whom for their embassy the Grecians chose,
To give Antenor and take back in trade
His daughter and King Thoas, as he prayed;
And when King Priam had safe-conduct sent,
To Troy the legates on their mission went.

The purpose of their embassy they told,
And Priam listened with attentive ear;
A parliament he bade the Trojans hold,
Which I but briefly need to dwell on here,
For with one voice the Trojans spoke out clear,
That they approved of this proposed exchange,
And all details were ready to arrange.

NOW Troilus was present in the place,
When Cressida was being bargained for,
At which it might be gathered from his face
That this request had touched him deep and sore;
Yet he in silence this disaster bore,
And lest his speech his secret should reveal,
Manfully strove his sorrow to conceal.

Thus full of anguish and of ghastly fear,
He waited what the other lords would say,
And if from their debate it should appear,
That Cressida from Troy must go away,
Two things he planned to do without delay,
Both save her honest name, and keep her still
In Troy, if strength availed thereto or skill.

For if she longer might not there abide,
Then naught was left for him except to die,
But Reason told him on the other side,
That first for her advice he must apply;
For if he brought her in the public eye,
She might complain his meddling had revealed
Their love, that otherwise had been concealed.

To this decision thus he came at last,
That if the lords decreed that she must go,
He would assent to any law they passed,
And then his lady seek and let her know,
And what she bade him do, he would do so,
Cost what it might in labor or in strife,
For what she willed, was dearer than his life.

NOW Hector, who had heard the Greeks' demand,
For Cressida Antenor to restore,
Against this spoke and firmly took his stand:
"Sirs, she is not a prisoner of war!
I know not what you want this lady for,
But for my part, you can go back and tell
Your friends, we have no women here to sell!"

You can't imagine what a stir this made,
For all the folk blazed up like straw on fire;
Their luck against them in this matter played,

They got their wish and their confusion dire.
"Hector," they said, "what's this that you require,
To shield this woman and cause us thus to lose
Antenor, whom you should the rather choose,

"Who is so wise and of such great renown,
And we have need of men, as you can see,
And he among the greatest in this town!
O Hector, let such foolish fancies be!
And Priam, king of Troy, hear our decree,
That we will have Antenor, yes or no,
And Cressida to her Greek friends may go!"

O JUVENAL, how truly thou didst say,
The people never know for what they seek,
For what they want seems right in every way,
And clouds of error ever render weak
Their judgments, in whate'er they do or speak;
For though Antenor now had every voice,
In time the Trojans shall repent their choice.

For later his own city he betrayed!
Alas, they brought him back to Troy too soon!
O foolish world, with error over-laid!
Poor harmless Cressida they now repugn,
And now her song of joy must change its tune,
For now to have Antenor all are bound,
And she must go, declare both hare and hound.

And so it was decreed in parliament,
At end of much debate and wild uproar,
And thus announced there by their president,
Though Hector did this action much deplore;
But finally he could do nothing more,
For folk and all in this were quite agreed,
And by the parliament it was decreed.

Discussion ended, home the Trojans went,
And Troilus, as well, with footsteps slow,
And then about their tasks his men he sent,
While he into his chamber straight did go;
But first he told his men, to hide his woe,
That he would rest and sleep an hour or two,
And on his lonely bed himself he threw.

And as the leaves in winter blow away,
By one and one, leaving the tree all bare,
And only bark and branch the winds withstay,
So now unhappy Troilus doth fare,
Close bound within the dismal bark of care,
And wild with fear lest he dare not refuse
The vote by which he Cressida must lose.

Then up he rose and fastened every door,
And window, too, and then this wretched man
Upon his bedside sat him down once more,
And sat as still as any image can,
And looked as wan, until his woe began
At last to break forth in a raging storm,
And how he acted, I shall you inform.

Not otherwise than as the fierce wild bull
Doth roar and leap and spring, when from his heart
The huntsman forth the fatal spear doth pull,
So Troilus doth from his bedside start,
And beat his breast, and here and yonder dart,
Striking his head full hard against the wall,
And to the floor his body oft doth fall.

His eyes for very sorrow turned to fountains,
From which the tears in double streamlets well,
And from his breast, as if from bursting mountains,
The sobs broke forth, scarce leaving breath to tell
His grief. "O death," he said, "thou traitor fell,
Why must I stay alive who curse the day
That I was born this hapless part to play!"

But when the fury and the blinding rage
Which thus his heart afflicted and oppressed,
With time began a little to assuage,
Upon his bed he laid him down to rest,
And now the flood of tears attained its crest;
It was a marvel that the body could
Endure the woe and grief in which he stood.

"O Fortune," he exclaimed, "alas the while!
What have I done? What crime have I committed?
How didst thou have the heart me to beguile?
Shall I by thee be evermore outwitted?

Must thou so strong 'gainst Cressida be pitted?
Alas, that thou, so cruel and unkind,
Shouldst towards me cherish such a hostile mind!

"To honor thee do I not ever strive,
Above the other Gods and powers all?
Why dost thou of my blessing me deprive?
O Troilus, well may mankind thee call
Most wretched of all wretches, who dost fall
To such a depth, in which thou must bewail
Lost Cressida, till thy last breath shall fail.

"Fortune, alas, was it for my delight
In love that I have lost thy favor high?
Why didst thou not my father in despite
Deprive of life, or let my brother die,
Or me myself, who on thee thus do cry?
I, cumber-world, whose happy days are sped,
Forever dying, yet never fully dead!

"If Cressida alone to me were left,
I'd care not, Fortune, what course you might steer!
But of my love you have me now bereft,
For 'tis your way, to keep man still in fear,
To rob him of the one he holds most dear.
You prove your strength by wanton violence,
And thus I'm lost, all hopeless of defence.

"O Lord of love! O very God on high!
Thou knowest best my heart and all my thought;
What shall I do my life to occupy,
If I forgo what I so dear have brought?
Since thou my love and me hast safely brought
Into thy hand, and both our hearts hast sealed,
How could thy act then ever be repealed?

"What shall I do? And shall I never master
The living torment and the cruel pain
Of this so unforeseen and great disaster?
Alone in solitude let me complain,
And never see it shine or see it rain,
But in the dark, like Oedipus of old,
End both my life and sorrows manifold!

"O weary spirit, wandering to and fro,
When wilt thou seek elsewhere a place of rest
And let this body to destruction go?
O lurking soul, fly forth from out thy nest!
Abandon this sad heart and weary breast,
And follow Cressida, thy lady dear,
For now thy proper home no more is here.

"O weary eyes, since all your bliss and joy
Was but in Cressida's reflected light,
What will ye do, since I cannot employ
You as I would, but weep out all your sight?
Since she is quenched who was my lamp so bright,
From this time forth, my eyes are but in vain,
And all their virtue can me nothing gain.

"O Cressida, my sovereign lady dear,
Unto this grieving soul that thus doth cry,
Who shall give comfort when thou art not here?
Alas, no one! But when my heart shall die,
My spirit straight to thee alone shall fly,
To serve thee as thy everlasting slave,
While I shall lie forgotten in my grave.

"O all ye lovers, high upon the wheel
Of Fortune set in joy and bliss secure,
God grant that ye may find your love of steel,
And may your joyous life full long endure;
And when ye come upon my sepulture,
Remember that your comrade resteth there,
For I loved, too, though sorrow was my share.

"O, old, enfeebled, mis-behaving man—
Calchas I mean—what wickedness led thee
To leave thy Troy and join the Grecian clan?
O Calchas, thou my fatal bane wilt be,
For thou wast born to be a curse to me!
O would that Jove would grant the happy hour
That thou wert here in Troy and in my power!"

A thousand sighs as hot as glowing embers
Forth from his breast in swift succession rise,
When thus his sorrows freshly he remembers;

And streams of burning tears break from his eyes,
The burden of his heart to signalize,
Till nature yielding to the heavy stress
Of grief, he lies in dim unconsciousness.

NOW Pandar likewise at the parliament
Had heard what every lord and burgess said,
And how with one opinion they assent
That Cressida should to the Greeks be led,
And straightway he completely lost his head;
So shocked he was, his wits went all astray,
And off to Troilus he rushed away.

A certain knight who kept the chamber door
Permitted him to enter in the room,
And Pandar, weeping silently but sore,
Slipped in the chamber, dark as any tomb,
And to the bed he went in silent gloom,
So deeply agitated and dismayed,
One word he could not summon to his aid.

His heart by pity and compassion torn,
He stands, and on his breast his arms doth fold,
And gazes thus on Troilus forlorn,
Whose face a dreadful thing is to behold;
And Pandar feels his very heart grow cold
At sight of him thus prostrate in despair
Whose great affliction he would gladly share.

And Troilus, reviving when he felt
That Pandar was come there with sympathy,
Began like snow against the sun to melt,
And down their cheeks the tears ran copiously
Of these two comrades in adversity;
Yet speechless stood they there, these weeping two,
Nor yet had thought of anything to do.

But finally this woful Troilus,
Half dead with sorrow, burst out in a roar,
And with a strangely sounding voice spoke thus,
Mid sobs and moans and other noises more:
"The world hath nothing now for me in store!
Hast thou not heard how by the parliament,
Away from Troy my Cressida is sent?"

And Pandar, ghastly now and pale of hue,
Most pitifully spoke and answered, "Yes!
Would God it were as false as it is true!
I've heard it all, and must it all confess!
This end, O how could any person guess!
Who would have thought with such a sudden fling
Fortune our joy to this sad end would bring!

"In all this world no creature ever saw
Ruin so sudden and so undesigned,
So strange and utterly beyond all law!
But every accident can't be divined—
So goes the world! This lesson here I find,
Let no man think that he's exceptional,
For Fortune will desert us one and all.

"But tell me why you thus beyond all reason
Lament and lie upon your bed supine,
For had you not your joy in its good season?
Give thanks for joy, yourself to loss resign!
But I that ne'er in love, as thou in thine
Hast prospered, nor ever knew a friendly eye,
'Tis I who might thus weep and wail and sigh!

"And here's another thing—I dare aver
This town is full of ladies round about,
Fairer indeed than any twelve like her;
And if you want me, I can pick one out,
Yes, more than one or two, without a doubt.
Be glad, therefore, my own dear chosen brother,
If she is lost, why, we can get another.

"The Lord forbid that you should never glance
At things which have not been your chief delight!
If one can sing, another well can dance!
One may be fair, another gay and bright,
And virtue lack of beauty may requite!
Each by her excellences should be measured,
For heroner and falcon both are treasured.

"As Zanzis wrote, who was so very wise,
A new love expediteth oft the old,
Adapt yourself as new conditions rise,
And ever on your heart maintain your hold;

No fire so hot but time will make it cold;
And since all pleasures are but accidental,
New accidents are nothing detrimental.

"For just as sure as day comes after night,
Some new love, some new task, or some new woe,
Or even seldom having her in sight,
These all assist affections old to go.
And one of these you're bound to have, you know,
For out of sight, she'll soon be out of mind,
Whereby new comfort you shall quickly find."

These wise and cheering words good Pandar spoke
To help his friend as helpless he there lay,
As one who any measures would invoke,
No matter how much nonsense he might say.
But Troilus did slight attention pay
To all this rigmarole or what it meant,
In one and out the other ear it went.

At last he said, as on his arm he leaned,
"This medicine and cure proposed by you,
Were well enough if I were but a fiend!
Be false to Cressida, to me so true!
That's something, Pandar, I shall never do!
But slay me rather here upon the spot
Than I should add this shame to my sad lot.

"I'll serve her still, for all your worldly lore,
To whom my heart is bound by every right,
And shall do so until I breathe no more!
That humble faith which I to her did plight,
That shall I keep, and faith with faith requite;
As her true man I'll be forever bound,
And serve no other on this whole world round.

"But when you say that others you can find
As fair as she, compare her not, I pray,
With any creature formed of human kind!
And Pandar dear, I've only this to say
To your advice, and that is plainly, Nay!
And therefore I politely must request
That you will let these other ladies rest.

"You counsel me that I should love another,
And start afresh, and Cressida let go!
That lies not in my power, friend and brother!
And if I could, I never would do so.
And if you play the ball thus to and fro,
Now in, now out, now new love ousting old,
What claim on love can you expect to hold!

"Indeed what you have said seems thus to me,
As you should tell one sick with ills severe,
Who seeks your aid in his adversity,
'Don't think of pain, and pain will disappear,'—
As though a stone dwelt in my bosom here!
Against all feeling you must me insure
Before such medicine can work a cure.

"Let life from out this wretched breast depart,
And with my life, let thus my sorrows end,
Yet Cressida shall hold me, soul and heart,
And down with Proserpina I shall wend,
When heaven this relief to me shall send,
And there I will eternally complain
The bitter woe that cleft us two in twain!

"But for that argument of yours so fine,
That resignation lighter grief should be
Because my lady one time has been mine
And we have known the meaning of felicity—
What nonsense! Trulier once you said to me,
His lot is worse who out of joy is thrown
Than his who never any joy hath known.

"But tell me, since you take it thus so light,
To change your love and pass aye to and fro,
Why have you never exercised this right,
And left the one who brings you naught but woe?
If love comes light, it may as lightly go!
Why do you not hunt up another love,
And from your heart the cruel old one shove?

"If you, who never yet in love fared well,
Forth from your heart your old love cannot drive,
Can I, who once in heaven's joy did dwell

In bliss as great as any man alive,
Can I forget, though earnestly I strive?
O Pandar, tell me where you went to school,
Who argue thus so futilely by rule!

"'Tis nothing, Pandar, all that you have said!
I know quite well, whatever may befall,
My soul must now be numbered with the dead!
O death, thou certain end of sorrows all,
Come now, nor bid me oftener on thee call;
For blessed is the death so long time sought
By which an end to pain and grief is brought.

"Time was when life on earth to me was sweet
And death a hateful need and danger dire,
But now his coming I would gladly greet,
For nothing in this world I more desire.
O death, O soul, with anguish set afire,
Let falling tears the flames of sorrow drench,
Or thy cold stroke this mortal fever quench.

"O thou, who slayest in such sundry ways,
Against men's wills, unsought, by day or night,
Grant this request to one who humbly prays:
Relieve this world of him who doth but blight
Existence with his sorrows infinite!
The time has come for me to leave this earth,
For fate hath made my life but little worth."

SALT tears the eyes of Troilus distil,
Like liquid from alembic falling fast,
And Pandar held his tongue and kept him still,
And downward to the ground his eyes he cast;
This silence, though, could not forever last,
And rather than his friend should pass away,
Pandar was minded something more to say.

"Good friend, since you thus dwell in great distress,
And since you find so much in me to blame,
Why don't you make an effort to redress
Your griefs, and strength and manhood thus proclaim?
Take her by force and hold her so! For shame!
Or either let her go in peace elsewhere,
Or keep her here and banish all your care!

"Are thou in Troy, and dost thou lack the nerve
To take a woman who's in love with thee,
And would love more if thou more shouldst deserve?
A greater folly never did I see!
Get up at once, and let thy weeping be,
And show thou art a man, with manly powers,
You'll see that Cressida shall still be ours."

To these words Troilus made answer soft
And said, "In truth, my friend and brother dear,
All this I've thought myself, reflecting oft,
And more indeed than you've suggested here;
But many reasons thereagainst appear,
Which I will tell, if you good heed will pay,
And then your own opinion you may say.

"You know this town is now involved in war
Because a woman was borne off by force,
And as things stand, 'twould cause a great uproar,
If to such methods I should have recourse;
I'm sure 'twould be a very fruitful source
Of blame, if I my father's act withstood,
Since she's to be exchanged for Troy's own good.

"I've also thought, of course with her consent,
To ask my father for her as a favor,
But that to treason were equivalent,
For never would he in his duty waver,
Since in so high a public place he gave her
As parliament, and hath the edict sealed,
Which for his son could scarcely be repealed.

"And I'm afraid my lady 'twould disturb
If by such violence I should her claim;
The tongue of the world is very hard to curb,
And it might seem a slander on her name,
And I would rather die than cause her shame.
Her honor I hold dearer in my sight
Than anything beneath the heavens bright.

"All hope is lost, for aught that I can see!
For true it is, that as her faithful knight,
Her honor still my first concern must be;
Such service do I owe to her of right.

Desire and Reason in me ever fight;
Desire insists, Let force control the day,
But Reason counsels quite the other way!"

He wept as though his tears would never cease,
And said, "Alas, what course shall I pursue?
For all the while I feel my love increase,
And hope grow less and less, as it must do,
Since my distress itself doth still renew.
O heart, why will you not break in my breast!
Alas, a lover's heart hath seldom rest!"

"YOU may," said Pandar, "as far as I'm concerned,
Let your heart break! But were I in so deep,
A man like you, I'd take her, if it turned
The whole town topsy-turvy in a heap.
The more they talked, the stiller you could keep,
And to their hearts' content, just let them shout,
For nine days always wears a wonder out.

"Don't get involved in reasonings too deep
Or precious. Help yourself the first of all!
If some must weep, then let the others weep!
You two are one, you need no aid to call;
Get up, she shall not go, whate'er befall!
For some small blame 'tis better to incur,
Than die here like a gnat and never stir.

"Don't call it force, but follow my advice;
Firm action I would call it at the most.
No doubt she'd think that you were over-nice
To let them send her to the Grecian host.
Remember, too, it is no idle boast
That fortune helps the brave in his emprise,
But from the coward wretch she ever flies.

"Your lady may at first a little grieve,
But peace with her you easily can make.
To tell the truth, I can't at all believe
That she the very least offence will take.
Why then should you in fear and trembling quake?
You know what Paris did—follow your brother;
What's good for one, is good, too, for another.

"And Troilus, this also here I swear,
If Cressida, as we indeed suppose,
An equal love and faith with you doth share,
She'll thank you if she can escape her foes,
No matter what disturbance from it grows;
But on the other hand, if she abandons you,
Then she is false and fickle, through and through.

"Take courage then, recall you are a knight!
True love, you know, hath no regard for law.
Exhibit now your valor and your might,
And stand not here in trembling and in awe,
While griefs and fears your very vitals gnaw.
Despise the world and all the planets seven,
And if you die a martyr, go to heaven!

"And for your aid, I'll faithfully stand by,
With all my kin, throughout the country round,
Though on the street like dogs we all shall lie,
Stricken with many a wide and bloody wound;
Whatever falls, your friend I shall be found.
But if you'd rather die here like a wretch,
Farewell, to hell the devil may you fetch!"

THESE vigorous words made Troilus revive;
"Enough," he cried, "I give my full assent.
You need no further urge me on, or strive
To speak in terms so stern and vehement.
For here I tell you fully my intent:
Abduct her, that is what I mean to do,
But only so if she consents thereto."

"Let that," said Pandar, "be as be it may!
Have you inquiries of her ever made?"
And Troilus could answer naught but "Nay."
"Well, then," said Pandar, "why are you afraid?
You don't know if she'd be at all dismayed
To be abducted! Why then all this fear,
Unless some angel told it in your ear?

"Get up, pretend that nothing has occurred,
And wash your face, and on the king attend;
He'll wonder why from you he hasn't heard.

Yourself from all surmise you must defend,
Or unexpected he may sometime send
For you. In sort, be glad, my brother dear,
You really haven't anything to fear.

"For I shall try to bring it so about,
Tonight you'll see your lady in some way,
And then you two can thresh the whole thing out,
And you can tell from what she has to say,
Just what part each of you must plan and play,
And so decide what action seems the best.
Farewell, for at this point I pause and rest."

SWIFT Rumor, which repeateth untrue things
With equal speed as she repeateth true,
Had flown through Troy, with ever-ready wings,
From man to man, to tell this marvel new,
How Calchas' daughter, fair and bright of hue,
By sentence passed in highest parliament,
Forth to her ancient father should be sent.

To Cressida arrived this dreadful news,
But on her father she had little thought,
Except he could go hang when he might choose;
And Jupiter she earnestly besought
To curse the hour which this bad luck had brought;
But if the news that thus came to her ear
Were true or not, she dared not ask for fear.

For she had set her heart and mind
On Troilus long since, so firm and fast,
That all the world her love might not unbind,
Or Troilus from out her bosom cast,
For she was his, as long as life shall last.
And thus distracted both by love and terror,
She scarce could tell the truth apart from error.

IT IS the common custom in each land
For ladies to indulge in calls polite,
And now there came to Cressida a band,
Both glad and sad, as seemed to them but right;
And with their gossipings unwelcome quite,
These ladies, who in hapless Troy did dwell,
They sat them down and said as I shall tell.

"O, I'm so glad," the one of them doth cry,
"That now your father you so soon shall see!"
Another said, "Indeed, so am not I,
For all too little now in Troy she'll be!"
"Indeed I hope," the third one said, "that she
Shall bring us happy peace on every side,
And when she goes, may heaven be her guide!"

These words, and other female blandishments,
She hears, but in her thoughts they have no share;
Another picture quite her heart presents,
Although in body she is sitting there.
God knows her thought and mind are placed elsewhere,
And Troilus alone her spirit sought,
For whom she had no words, but all her thought.

These ladies with no wish but how to please,
Their breath in idle gossiping expend,
Wherein poor Cressida can find no ease,
Nor with her burning heart thereto attend
Scarce long enough a courteous ear to lend;
She felt that she was ready to expire,
With all this talk that doth her bore and tire.

And in the end, she might no more restrain
Her tears, for upward they began to well
As signs of all the inward bitter pain
In which her wretched spirit now must dwell,
Reflecting from what heaven to what hell
She fallen was, since she hath lost the joy
That she had known with Troilus in Troy.

And all the silly fools that sat about
Supposed she wept and sighed so long and sore,
Because from Troy she soon must now set out,
And their society enjoy no more!
And all the ladies there, almost a score,
They saw her weep, and loved her tender heart,
And in the weeping all of them took part.

And all endeavored with her to condole,
But little knew the things of which she thought,
Or what alone could cheer her and console;
And to be glad they often her besought,

Which to her grief such mitigation brought
As for a splitting headache one might feel
If one were kindly rubbed upon the heel.

WHEN they had said all they could think to say,
They took their leave and home departed all,
And Cressida, oppressed with sad dismay,
Into her chamber went from out the hall,
And like one dead, upon her bed doth fall,
Borne down by all this heavy weight of grief,
From which she saw no prospect of relief.

The bitter tears from out her eyes down pour,
Like April showers falling full and fast;
Her breast so white she beat, and evermore
She called on death to take her at the last,
Such heavy sorrow now her soul harassed,
Her lover lost, who was her only hope,
Forlorn in black despair so left to grope.

Her rippling hair, as golden as the sun,
She tore, and wrung her hands with fingers small,
But no relief from sorrow thus she won,
Nor yet from death, on whom she oft doth call;
Her hue so bright lay hidden neath a pall,
In testimony of this hard distraint,
And thus with sobs she uttered this sad plaint:

"Alas, sent forth from out my home and nation,
I, woful wretch, bereft of all delight,
And born beneath a cursed constellation,
Must now depart from my beloved's sight!
Woe worth the day, and specially the night,
When first I saw him with my eyes so plain,
Who causes me, as I cause him, such pain!

"What shall he do? And what indeed shall I?
How shall I now my life anew begin?
And O, dear heart, for whom I'd gladly die,
Who shall relieve the sorrow you are in?
O Calchas, father, thine is all this sin!
I curse the day my mother dear, Argive,
Brought me into this wretched world alive!

"To what end should I live and sorrow thus?
Shall fishes without water long endure?
What worth is Cressida if Troilus
Is gone? For must not every plant procure
Its proper food, existence to assure?
Many a time I've heard the old wives say,
'Withdrawn from earth, things green all pass away.'

"And now, since either sword or pointed dart
Would be a rather cruel end for me,
The day that I from Troilus depart,
If simple grief my slayer will not be,
From that day on, all food and drink I'll flee,
Until my soul shall breathe its final breath,
Starvation bringing me a welcome death.

"And Troilus, let me be dressed in black,
In tokening, my precious sweetheart dear,
That I am gone and never can come back,
Who once was all your consolation here.
And so I'll live, till I lie on my bier,
As one from whom joy doth itself absent,
In sorrow, solitude and deep lament.

"My heart and soul and all that dwells therein,
Bequeath I with your spirit to remain
Eternally, for each is other's twin.
And though on earth we parted were in twain,
Yet in that blessed field, all freed from pain,
Where Pluto rules, we shall together be,
As Orpheus was with his Eurydice.

"Thus, sweetheart, by a stern decree of state,
Troy must I leave and with the Greeks abide,
And how canst thou survive this dreadful fate?
Why should this grief your tender heart betide?
But sweetheart mine, forget this woe so wide,
And me as well! For truly I can say,
If you are happy, let me go my way!"

Who might, as I cannot, the tale have sung
Which plaintively she made of her distress?
But as for me and for my feeble tongue,

In that attempt, I'd have such slight success
'Twould make her sorrows seem far less
Than they should seem, and weakly would I show
Her high lament, and so I let it go.

As emissary sent by Troilus
To Cressida, as you have heard me say,
And as before it was agreed on thus,
The first step in the plans that they would lay,
Came Pandar now, by some quite secret way,
Prepared his message wholly to explain
To her reclined upon her couch of pain.

Poor Cressida, she was a woful sight,
Her breasts tear-stained with falling drops that made
Their way unheeded down her cheeks so white!
Her golden hair in bright disorder strayed
About her ears, escaped from out its braid,
Undoubted signal of the martyrdom
Of death, which none too soon for her may come.

At sight of him, she strove for shame anon
Her tearful face behind her arms to hide,
At which good Pandar was so woe-begone,
He scarcely in the chamber might abide,
At her sad look he was so horrified;
And now her flood of woe broke out anew
And by release a thousandfold it grew.

Then thus with words to sorrow she gave voice:
"My uncle Pandar, cause of causes first
That in the light of love I did rejoice,
My joy to sudden woe is now reversed!
Shouldst thou be welcomed here or be accursed,
Who thus hast guided me in love's emprise,
To end, alas, in this so wretched wise!

"Must love then end in woe? Yes, or men lie,
And every worldly joy, it seems to me,
For grief the place of joy must occupy!
And he who doubts if such the end must be,
Let him behold my grievous fate and see
How I from bad must ever pass to worse,
And thus am led my hateful birth to curse.

"Who looks at me, beholdeth sorrows all,
All pain, all torture, woe and all distress;
I have no need on other harms to call,
As anguish, languor, cruel bitterness,
Discomfort, dread, and madness more and less;
Methinks from heaven above the tears must rain
In pity for my harsh and cruel pain."

"I GRANT, dear lady, that your lot is hard,"
Said Pandar, "yet what do you plan to do?
For to yourself you should have more regard,
And not some vain and useless course pursue;
But now I want to say a word or two—
A message I must briefly now present
From Troilus, whose heart with pain is rent."

Her face she turned to him, so deathly pale,
It was a most distressing sight to see.
"Alas," she said, "can words for aught avail?
What can my precious sweetheart say to me
Since we are lost through all eternity?
Will he have news of all the tears I've shed?
They are enough, at least that can be said."

Her grief exacts from her a dreadful price,
She looks like one to her last bier consigned;
Her face, the image once of Paradise,
Is changed completely to another kind.
The play, the laughter men were wont to find
In her, and all her varied wit renewed,
Have fled, and left her mute in solitude.

About her eyes there stands a purple ring,
A silent token of her grief and pain,
Wherein to gaze was a distressing thing,
And Pandar was unable to restrain
His tears, which from his eyes began to rain;
But still things couldn't last forever thus,
And soon he spoke to her for Troilus:

"You know, dear niece, that it is sadly true,
The king and other lords have thought it best
To take Antenor in exchange for you,
From which comes all this woe and this unrest;

And how all this doth Troilus molest,
It is beyond the power of human tongue
To tell, such deadly grief his heart hath wrung.

"For this we both have sorrowed, he and I,
And both have felt the pangs of mortal pain,
But through my counsel he at length doth try
Somewhat from useless weeping to abstain;
And now, it seems, that Troilus would fain
Be all night with you in convenient wise,
Some remedy to plan and to devise.

"Of this I've come you briefly to inform,
If I his message rightly comprehend,
And you, who now indulge in such a storm
Of grief, may wisely to his words attend,
And back to him a proper answer send;
But let me ask above all things, my dear,
Leave off these tears ere Troilus comes here."

"Great is my grief," she said, still sighing sore,
As one who felt the pangs of dire distress,
"Yet his great sorrow grieves me even more,
And by comparison, mine seems the less.
Alas, that love and woe together press
Upon his heart, where joy cannot remain!
The grief he feels doth double all my pain.

"God knows 'tis hard from him to separate,
But harder yet than this it is to know
That he is suffering in such sorrow great!
The thought alone the chill of death doth blow
Upon my heart and sorrows new there grow.
Then bid him come, or in his stead let death
Drive out my soul and its last lingering breath!"

BURYING her face within her arms, she gave
Herself again to tears most copiously.
"O now," said Pandar, "why can't you behave
More sensibly? A moment or two and he
Will come, and what a sight then will he see?
I would not have him find you thus in tears,
'Twould add too much to all his other fears.

"For if he knew you took things in this way,
He'd kill himself, and so he must not know;
I'd never let him come here, night or day,
For all the wealth that Priam could bestow!
Were he here now, I know how things would go!
To what I say, I beg you then attend,
These tears and cries you must bring to an end.

"Strive rather now his sorrow to relieve
And not to magnify it, dearest niece;
Hard measures will not joy retrieve,
But soft and gentle ways will bring you peace.
What use are tears, though tears should never cease,
And you were drowned in them? Far better sure
Than tears are all the happy means of cure.

"Now, my advice is, when your plans are made,
Since you are wise and both of one assent,
Arrange for your departure to evade,
Or quick return, if that you can't prevent.
Women do best without long argument,
Let's see now what your woman's wit avails,
And I'll be there to help you when it fails."

"Go then," said Cressida, "and truly I
Shall do my best all weeping to restrain
While he is here, and earnestly shall try
To make him glad, and free him of his pain,
Through all his heart in every coursing vein.
If any salve for him I can discover,
I shall be found not lacking to my lover."

THEN Pandar went, and Troilus he sought,
And found him in a temple all alone,
Weary of life and much in mind distraught,
And there he prayed and made his bitter moan,
And of his prayers, this was the constant tone,
That end of life might bring him end of grief,
For well he thought this was his sole relief.

And in his mind, the simple truth to tell,
He was so fallen in despair that day,
He thought no longer in this world to dwell,

And argued of it in the following way:
"I am," he said, "but done for, so to say;
For all that comes, comes by necessity,
Thus to be done for is my destiny.

"I must believe and cannot other choose,
That Providence, in its divine foresight,
Hath known that Cressida I once must lose,
Since God sees everything from heaven's height
And plans things as he thinks both best and right,
According to their merits in rotation,
As was arranged for by predestination.

"But still I don't quite know what to believe!
For there have been great scholars, many a one,
Who say that destined fate we must receive,
Yet others prove that this need not be done,
And that free choice hath been denied to none
Alack, so sly they are, these scholars old,
I can't make out what doctrine I should hold!

"For some declare, what God perceives before,
(And God of course can never be misled)
All that must be, though men may it deplore,
Because foreordination hath so said;
Wherefore the thought still lingers in my head,
If God foreknows the thought and act of each
Of us, we have no choice, as scholars preach.

"For neither thought nor deed might ever be,
Or anything, unless foreordination,
In which there may be no uncertainty,
Perceives it without shade of variation;
For if there were the slightest hesitation
Or any slip in God's foreordering,
Foreknowledge then were not a certain thing,

"But rather one would call it expectation,
Unsteadfast, not foreknowledge absolute;
And that, indeed, were an abomination,
For God's foreknowledge thus to substitute
Imperfect human doubts and mere repute;
In God such human error to imply
Were false and foul and cursed treason high.

"Then there is this opinion held by some,
Whose tonsured foreheads quite imposing shine;
They say whatever happens does not come
Because foreknowledge sees with fixed design
That come it must, but rather they incline
To say that come it will, and reason so,
That such foreknowledge doth but merely know.

"But there resides here a perplexity
That in some proper way must be explained,
That things that happen do not have to be
Merely because they may be foreordained;
Yet still this truth at least must be maintained,
That all the things that ever shall befall,
Must surely be ordained, both one and all.

"You see that I am trying to find out
Just what is cause and what is consequence.
Is God's foreknowledge cause beyond a doubt
As necessary in his plain prepense
Of all the human things we call events,
Or does necessity in them reside
And thus ordaining cause for them provide?

"I must confess I can't pretend to show
Just how the reasons stand, but this I'll say,
That every thing that happens, must do so,
And must have been foreknown in such a way
That made it necessary, though it may
Be that foreknowledge did not so declare
That it must happen, be it foul or fair.

"But if a man is sitting on a chair,
Then this necessity you can't evade,
That true it is that he is sitting there,
And thus a truthful judgment you have made;
And furthermore against this may be laid
A supplement to this and its contrary,
As thus—pray heed, and just a moment tarry.

"I say if that opinion which you hold
That he sits there is true, then furthermore
He must be sitting there, as I have told;
There's thus necessity on either score,

That he must sit, as we agreed before,
And you must think he does and so say I,
Necessity on both of you doth lie.

"But you may urge, this man, he does not sit
Because your judgment on this may be true,
But rather, since he sat ere you thought it,
Your judgment from his sitting doth ensue;
But I say, though your judgment may be due
To his first sitting there, necessity
To judge and sit distributed must be.

"These arguments I think I may advance,
And make apply, for so it seems to me,
To God's foreknowledge and foreordinance,
In all the happenings that come to be.
And by these arguments you well may see,
That all the things that on the earth befall,
By plain necessity they happen all.

"Though things to come must all be foreordained,
Their cause therein you cannot simply find,
For these two points apart must be maintained,
But yet foreordinance cannot be blind,
And God must foreordain with truthful mind,
Or else whatever foreordained should be,
Would come to pass through blind necessity.

"But no more arguments I need display
To show that free choice is an idle dream.
Yet this, however, 'tis quite false to say,
That temporal things one should esteem
As cause of God's foreknowledge aye supreme;
From such opinion only errors grow,
That things that happen cause him to foreknow.

"I must suppose then, had I such a thought,
That God ordains each thing that is to come
Because it is to come, and for else naught!
Why, then, I might believe things, all and some,
From ages past, whate'er they issued from,
Are cause of God's high power that before
Hath known all things and nothing doth ignore!

"I have just one more point to add hereto,
That when I know that there exists a thing,
I know my knowing of that thing is true,
And so, whatever time to pass shall bring,
Those things I know must come; the happening
Of things foreknown ere their appointed hour,
Can be prevented by no human power.

"Almighty Jove, supreme upon thy throne,
O thou who knowest all things false and true,
In pity let me perish here alone,
Or Cressida and me no more pursue
With woe!" He paused, and scarcely was he through
With this request, when Pandar doth appear
Within the door, and speaks as you shall hear.

"ALMIGHTY Jove," he echoed, "on thy throne,
Who ever saw a grown man acting so?
Can't you do something else than weep and moan?
Why, Troilus, you are your own worst foe!
Good heavens, Cressida may never go,
So why afflict yourself with needless dread
And almost cry your eyes out of your head?

"Recall how many years you've lived, dear brother,
Without her, yet you got along with ease!
You weren't made for her and nary other!
There's plenty more who know the art to please.
Among your helpful thoughts you might place these,
That as the chance in dice falls when you throw,
Just so in love, your pleasures come and go.

"But this to me is cause of great surprise,
That you disturb your soul, and yet don't know,
Touching her going, what in the future lies,
Nor if she can't devise some way to throw
Them off the track, and so not need to go;
To meet the ax a man his neck may stretch,
But why should that give pleasure to the wretch?

"And now I'll tell you what I have to say.
I've been with her and told her your petition,
As we agreed between ourselves today,

And Troilus, I have a shrewd suspicion,
That in her heart she's got a proposition,
Though what it was she didn't fully mention,
That will repay the carefullest attention.

"And so, if you'll take my advice, tonight
Just go to her and bring this to an end,
For blessed Juno, through her ample might,
Shall, as I hope, her favor to us send.
I'm quite convinced your lady will attend
To this affair, so set your mind at rest,
For all at last will turn out for the best."

Troilus replied, as Pandar reached the door,
"Perhaps you're right, I might as well do so—"
Although, of course, he said a great deal more,
And when the time arrived for him to go,
Most secretly, so not a soul should know,
He came to her, as he was wont to do
Their usual occupations to pursue.

And truly at the first, when there they meet,
Sorrow about their hearts doth wind and twist,
So neither may in words the other greet,
But each in other's arms, each other kissed;
Thus silently they keep this mournful tryst,
For gathering woe in both their hearts so throbs,
No words can find a place among their sobs.

The precious tears that there descend and fall
Were bitter tears, of an unnatural kind,
As though of aloes mingled or of gall.
The woful Myrrha wept through bark and rind
No tears like these, as I her story find.
In all this world, no heart could be so hard
For such despair to lack as deep regard.

But when their wandering weary spirits twain
Returned were to the hearts where they should dwell,
And long lament had lightened so their pain,
When, too, the bitter tears ebbed in their well,
And less the sorrows in their bosoms swell,
To Troilus then Cressida thus spoke,
With hoarse and halting voice that often broke:

"O Jove! O God! Thy mercy I beseech!
Help, Troilus!" And therewithal her face
Upon his breast she laid, bereft of speech,
Her woful spirit ready to retrace
Its course back to its starting place;
And thus she lies, her face all pale and green,
Though fairest once, and freshest to be seen.

And Troilus, who doth her thus behold,
Calling her name to wake her from the dead,
And feeling all her limbs grow stiff and cold,
And both her eyes cast upward in her head,
This Troilus was filled with mortal dread,
And many a time her lips so cold he kissed,
And prayed the Gods with comfort to assist.

Her body on her couch he straightly laid,
For now her cheeks with life no longer glow;
Good reason now has he to be dismayed,
And now his song is but a song of woe.
For when he saw her lying speechless so,
With voice and tears and sobs together blended,
He cried, "Her sorrows are at last all ended!"

From loud lament he could not be restrained,
And wrung his hands and said what was to say
And on his heaving breast the salt tears rained;
But finally his tears he wiped away,
And for her flitting soul he thus doth pray:
"O God, established on thy throne above,
Grant me that I shall follow soon my love!"

HOW cold she was, how robbed of all sensation,
Nor trace of tender breathing could he feel,
Which was for him the final declaration,
As there beside her he did sadly kneel,
That she had suffered now the last ordeal;
And so the body of his lady dear
He placed as one does bodies for the bier.

And after this, with sternly hardened heart,
His shining sword from out its sheath he drew,
To slay himself and from this life to part,
So that his soul might quickly hers pursue,

And both receive from Minos judgment due,
Since love and cruel fortune so decide
That he may in this world no longer bide.

His life resigned, he voiced his high disdain:
"O cruel Jove, and Fortune so adverse,
I can but say that falsely ye have slain
My love, and since ye can do nothing worse,
Your might and all your evil works I curse!
Ye shall naught in this coward fashion gain,
For death shall never separate us twain!

"Now all this world, since ye have slain her thus,
I here renounce, and after her will hie;
No lover true shall say that Troilus
To share his lady's death did e'er deny.
Together to one fate we two will fly,
And since ye will not suffer us to live,
One stroke of death to our two spirits give!

"And O thou city, where I live in woe,
And Priam, and my brothers dwelling here,
And thou, my mother, farewell, for I go!
And Atropos, make ready now my bier!
And blessed Cressida, my sweetheart dear,
Receive my soul!"—he was about to say,
With sword at heart, prepared himself to slay,

But, thanks to God, she woke up from her swoon,
And drew a breath, and "Troilus!" she sighed,
And "Sweetheart, Cressida!" he answered soon,
"Are you alive?" and let his weapon slide;
"Yes, sweetheart, thanks to Venus!" she replied,
And therewithal a mighty sigh she heaved,
And Troilus now felt somewhat relieved.

He took her in his arms and kissed her oft,
To make her glad was now his sole intent,
Until her spirit, flickering aye aloft,
Again into its harbor softly went;
But then it chanced, her glances sidelong bent,
His sword upon the floor she did espy,
As it lay bare, which drew from her a cry.

She asked him why his sword he thus had drawn,
And Troilus the reason straightway told,
How he would slay himself therewith anon;
And she with wide eyes doth her knight behold
And him in arms most lovingly enfold;
"O mercy God! What an escape!" she cried,
"Alas, 'twere little but we both had died!

"And if I hadn't spoken, by good chance,
You would have slain yourself with it?" asked she;
"Quite right!" he answered with a loving glance,
And she replied, "By Him who fashioned me,
I would not living on this planet be
After thy death, if I were crowned the queen
Of all the land the sun hath ever seen.

"But straight thy very bloody sword I'd seize
And after thee, myself I'd slay! But ho!
Enough of such sad possibilities!
Arise and straight to bed now let us go,
Where we can peacefully discuss our woe.
For by the night-light now so lowly burning,
I know the day is not far from returning."

THOUGH in her bed reclined in love's embrace,
Unlike was this to nights that went before,
For sadly they behold each other's face
As though their joy was flown forevermore,
And their misfortune often they deplore.
But Cressida at last took things in hand,
And thus to him her thoughts she did expand:

"Lo, sweetheart, this you know most certainly,
That if a man does nothing but complain,
And seeks no way from trouble to be free,
That is but folly and increase of pain;
And since we've come together here, we twain,
To find a way out of the way we're in,
It seems to me it's high time to begin.

"I'm but a woman, as of course you know,
But my opinion I will tell you free
And frank, just as it comes in its first glow,

That neither you nor I, it seems to me,
Need get excited in such high degree,
Because there must be some way of redress
For all this wrong that causes us distress.

"As it now stands, the thought that we most hate,
The thought that robs us of all hope of bliss,
Is merely that we two must separate,
And all in all, there's nothing more amiss!
And what is then the remedy for this?
But that we manage soon again to meet!
That's all there is to it, my precious sweet!

"Now that I certainly can bring about,
To come back soon again if I must go,
Of this I do not have the slightest doubt,
For at the most within a week or so,
I shall be back, and now I shall you show,
Just briefly, and in simple words and few,
How I shall carry my proposal through.

"But I don't want to make a long discourse,
For time once lost cannot recovered be,
And if you'll only trust to my resource,
'Twill be the best, as soon I think you'll see.
And, sweetheart, pray you now, forgive it me,
If what I say, seems somewhat hard to you,
For truly, 'tis the best that we can do.

"So let me here most earnestly protest
That the intent of all that I shall say
Is but to show what I regard the best,
And I believe, in fact the only way
To help ourselves—and take it so, I pray!
But in the end, whatever you require,
That will I do—it is my sole desire.

"Now listen! You of course will understand,
I go away by act of parliament,
And both of us must yield to that command.
There is no earthly way to circumvent
This act, and thus we may as well assent,
And so with that, dismiss it from our mind
And look about some better way to find.

"Of course it's true, the parting of us twain
Most dreadfully will both of us annoy;
But every lover must endure some pain,
Or he would not appreciate his joy.
And since I go no farther out of Troy
Than I can ride again in half a morrow,
There's not much reason here to grieve or sorrow.

"For sure the Greeks will not me so immure,
But day by day, my darling sweetheart dear,
(You know this truce for some time will endure),
Of all my doings you shall fully hear.
And ere the truce is o'er, I'll reappear;
If you will keep an eye on your demeanor,
You shall have me, and Troy shall have Antenor!

"And think, 'What though my Cressida is gone,
'Twill not be long before she's back again.'"
"But when, alas!" "I swear it, right anon,
Or maybe several days, or nine or ten.
And when I come, you'll be so happy then,
That we shall evermore together dwell,
In greater bliss than all the world can tell.

"You know with things arranged as they are now,
We're oft compelled our private life to hide,
And dare no trysts or conference allow—
A fortnight thus our patience oft is tried—,
And can't you then a mere ten days abide,
My honest reputation to insure?
Of course you can, or yet much more endure!

"And don't forget that all my kin are here,
Except my father, who of course is not,
And all my property, which I hold dear,
And thou, dearer than all the wealth I've got,
Whom I would not exchange for any lot
On all this earth, so wide as earth hath space,
I swear it in the sight of great Jove's face!

"Do you suppose my father, who is wise,
Desires to see me, but that he's afraid
Lest folk mistrust me here or me despise,
Because of all the trouble he has made?

But why should he suppose I need his aid?
If he knew how content I am in Troy,
He would his wits in other ways employ.

"You see, besides, how each day more and more
Men treat of peace, and everywhere they say
The Trojans will Queen Helen soon restore
And then the Greeks will quickly sail away,
And that will be for us a blessed day;
And so you may with ease of heart abide,
Because they treat of peace on either side.

"And when the peace shall come, my sweetheart dear,
You know the town and place will be alive
With Grecian messengers who will come here,
And some will go and new ones will arrive,
As thick as honey-bees about a hive,
And everyone will then be free to go
Wherever he will, and no one care or know.

"And even though the plans for peace fall through,
I must come back, for could I anywhere
Or either go or stay away from you?
And I could never stand it living there
Within a camp devoted to warfare;
And so if you regard what I have said,
I don't see why you need have any dread.

"But I've another plan that's sure to hold
If what I've spoken of should not suffice.
My father Calchas is now growing old,
And greed you know, is still an old man's vice.
And if I wanted to, I could entice
Him to our net, and I dare make the vaunt
That we shall have him doing what we want.

"'Tis hard, so doth the ancient proverb go,
To fill the wolf and hold intact the sheep,
Which is to say, that often men must throw
Away a part, if they the rest will keep.
With gold it's very easy to cut deep
Into the heart of him who's set on gain,
And what I plan to do, I'll now explain.

"The ready cash I have here in this town,
I'll take it to my father and I'll say,
'Tis sent to him by friends to salt it down
And keep it safe against a rainy day,
And that these friends most fervently do pray
Him send for more, and the first chance embrace,
Because this town is such a risky place.

"And what's to come shall be a huge amount—
So shall I say—and lest it be espied,
It must be sent by me on their account;
And then I'll show him, that if peace betide,
What friends I have at court on every side,
Who Priam's wrath will help to mitigate
And him in Trojan favor reinstate.

"So what for all the things I'll to him tell,
I'll so enchant him, as I said before,
He'll think he doth in heaven surely dwell.
That for Apollo, or for his clerkly lore,
Or for his calculations by the score!
Desire for gold shall so his priestcraft blind,
I shall him 'round my finger lightly wind.

"And if he puts to test by priestly skill
If I am lying, I'll pull him by the sleeve
And in his divinations doubt instil,
So that at last I'll lead him to believe
The oracles he wrongly doth receive.
The Gods all speak in amphibologies,
And twenty times more lies than truths in these.

"Fear made the Gods at first, so shall I say,
And now again that same fear in his heart
Made him report their omens the wrong way,
When he in fear from Delphi did depart.
You'll see that I shall give him such a start
That he will turn completely round about;
Within a day or two, you'll find this out."

I CAN but think, as I it written find,
That all of this was said with good intent,
And that her heart withal was true and kind,

And what she said, all that she truly meant,
And of her grief no part did she invent,
And ever thought to him she would be true,
But of her heart, not all of it she knew.

Poor Troilus, with heart and ears outspread,
Drank in this tale of plotting to and fro,
And almost was convinced by what she said,
But nevertheless to let her from him go,
That gave him many a pang of doubt and woe;
But finally, against his better mind,
He trusted her and all his doubts resigned.

The tempest of his grief somewhat abated,
Despair gave way to hope, and new delight
Of love was for old sorrow reinstated;
And as the birds against the sun so bright
Sing on the branch, though hidden from all sight,
So were their words to this so loving pair
Songs of delight, their solace to declare.

Yet still the thought that Cressida must go,
Troilus could not drive from out his mind,
And all his words his dark forebodings show
That truth in her he might not ever find;
"If e'er to me," he said, "you are unkind,
And if you come not on your day to town,
Farewell my health, my honor and renown!

"For just as sure as morrow's sun shall rise,
If your returning you should long delay,
No other refuge open to me lies,
But black despair at once my heart will slay;
And though the thought of death brings no dismay,
Rather than such grief on us both should fall,
Sweetheart, I beg, don't go away at all!

"To tell the truth, my precious sweetheart dear,
Those little tricks of yours of which you've told,
They fill me not with hope, but ghastly fear.
'The bear thinks of one thing,' goes the saying old,
'Although his leader other views may hold!'
Your sire is wise, you must look out for it,
'One may the wise outrun, but not outwit.'

"It's very hard to limp and not be spied
Before a cripple—that's his specialty.
In tricks your father sure is Argus-eyed,
And though his gold took wings and forth did flee,
His cunning still is left in full degree.
You won't fool him, for all your woman's ways,
And grave doubts in my mind you merely raise.

"I do not know if peace shall e'er be made,
But peace or no, it's really all the same,
For Calchas by his turning renegade
Hath so besmirched and so defiled his name,
He dare not come to Troy again for shame,
And so that plan, so far as I can see,
Is nothing but a pleasing fantasy.

"You'll see—your father shall you so persuade,
You'll marry there, for he knows how to preach;
For some fine Greek he'll have his plans well laid,
And carry you away with his soft speech,
Or make you wed by force, his end to reach;
And Troilus may then go hang forsooth,
For all his innocence and all his truth!

"Yet more—your father doth us all despise,
And says our city is but lost and lorn,
That from this siege we never shall arise,
Since all the Greeks most solemnly have sworn
We shall be slain, and down our walls be torn;
Such fearsome words he will unto you say,
That in the end among the Greeks you'll stay!

"And you will see so many a lusty knight
Among the Greeks, and of such mansuetude,
And each of them with heart and wit and might
To please you well abundantly imbued,
That soon you'll weary of the manners rude
Of simple Trojans, loosing from your mind
The bonds that our two hearts together bind.

"And this to me so grievous is to think,
That from my breast the very soul 'twill rend,
To lowest depths I feel my heart doth sink,
But at the thought that you from Troy will wend;

Against your father's cunning, heaven defend!
So if you go away, as I have said,
You may as well count me among the dead.

"So now, with humble, true and faithful heart,
A thousand times your pardon here I pray;
Regard the matter, sweetheart, from my part,
And do somewhat as I shall to you say,
And let us two in silence steal away;
Bethink 'tis naught but folly pure and plain,
To lose the great, some minor point to gain.

"I mean that since we may, ere break of day,
Steal forth and be together ever so,
What need for such uncertainty to stay,
If you hence to the Grecian army go,
Of your returning here again or no?
Why should we put in pawn a joy secure
For far-off prospects, doubtful and unsure?

"And now to speak of low, material things
Like money, each of us can take along
Enough to buy what pleasures money brings,
Till death shall take us with his power strong.
This do I urge, this choice cannot be wrong,
With any other plan or other plea,
I cannot in my heart or mind agree.

"Of poverty you need have not a fear,
For I have hosts of kin and friends elsewhere,
And though in our bare shirts we did appear,
In all their gold and gear they'd give us share,
And honor us the while we rested there.
So let us go, and go without delay,
I wait but till the happy word you say!"

CRESSIDA paused, and said with many sighs,
"In very truth, my precious sweetheart true,
We might thus steal away, as you advise,
Or try some other thriftless plans and new,
But afterward we would it surely rue,
And let me say again, as I have said,
There is no ground for all your fear and dread.

"If it should come, at any day or hour,
Through fear of parent or of other wight,
For rank or pride or thought of marriage dower,
That I am false, my Troilus, my knight,
Let Juno, Saturn's daughter, through her might,
Send me, as mad as Athamas, to dwell
Eternally in Styx, the pit of hell!

"And this I swear, by every God supernal,
And swear it, too, by every bright Goddess,
By every Nymph and Deity infernal,
By every Faun and Satyr, more and less,
Those demi-gods that haunt the wilderness,
That Atropos may snip her fatal shears
If I am false or justify your fears!

"Thou, Simois, that like an arrow clear
Through Troy aye runnest downward to the sea,
Bear witness of the pledge that I speak here,
And on the day that I untrue shall be
To Troilus, who holds my heart in fee,
Flow backward tothy primal source and well,
And let me soul and body sink to hell!

"What you propose, to slip away and go,
And leave your friends, a lonely life to lead,
No woman should induce you to do so,
Especially as Troy hath now such need
Of help; and of another thing take heed,
If this were known, the state would have my life,
And death dishonored end all earthly strife.

"And if sometime the armies should make peace,
For wildest moments must give way to tame,
Your lamentations then would never cease,
Because you couldn't come back here for shame;
And so before you peril thus your name,
Be not too hot, or on rash action bent;
The hasty man must many times repent.

"What think you all the people round about
Would say of it? 'Tis easy to surmise!
They'd say, and think it true beyond a doubt,

Not love impelled you to such enterprise,
But lust and coward fear, and such like lies.
And thus were lost, sweetheart so dear,
Your honest name, which shines now bright and clear.

"And also think a moment on my name,
Flourishing yet, but with how dark a blot
And with what stains it would be brought to shame,
If I should flee to some forbidden spot;
Never till death should end my mortal lot
Could I again fair reputation win;
Thus were I lost, and lost in shame and sin.

"Let rashness then to reason make way here!
Men say, 'To patience comes the victory,'
And, too, 'Who will be dear, he must hold dear.'
Thus make a virtue of necessity!
Be patient! Think that fortune's lord is he
Who asks no help from her in his pursuits;
The coward wretch alone she persecutes.

"Believe, sweetheart, with perfect confidence,
Before Lucina, Phoebus' sister dear,
Her path beyond the Lion shall commence,
Without a doubt again I shall be here—
I mean that when the tenth day shall appear,
No power short of death can so prevail
To make me in my promised coming fail."

"SO MUST it be," said Troilus at last,
"And since I must, I will await that day,
For well I see, time of debate is past!
But for the love of God, once more I pray,
Let us tonight in secret steal away,
Together forever, forever so at rest,
The counsels of the heart are ever best."

"O now," cried Cressida distressedly,
"Alas, you drive me wild with all your fears!
It seems you have but little trust in me,
And by your words it patently appears!
In Cynthia's name, so bright among the spheres,
Mistrust me not, for thou hast little reason
To lay against me any taint of treason.

"Bethink you well that often it is art
To lose some time a better time to gain,
And though we for a day or two must part,
I'm not yet lost, nor shall I lost remain,
And from such foolish thoughts, I beg, refrain.
Now trust in me and banish all this sorrow,
Or grief will end my days before tomorrow.

"For if you knew how much I am oppressed
By this, you'd cease your argument;
The very spirit weepeth in my breast
To hear you grieve and bitterly resent
That with the Greeks a few days must be spent!
Though I myself, did I not know the cure,
Such fate with fortitude could not endure.

"But I am not of such a simple mind
That I can't ferret out some easy way,
A speedy time for my return to find,
For who can hold what hath a will to stray?
My father can't, whatever tricks he play!
And take it so, my going forth from Troy
But antecedent is to greater joy!

"With all my heart I therefore you beseech,
If anything you'll ever grant to me,
And for the love that we have each for each,
Ere from my presence you tonight must flee,
A smile upon your features I may see,
As cheering witness to my troubled breast
That once again our hearts in union rest.

"And finally," she said, "one thing I pray,
My soul's delight and only satisfaction,
Since I am wholly thine, while I'm away,
Seek not elsewhere for pleasure and distraction,
Nor let love grow oblivious from inaction!
For still I fear, since often it is said,
'In love there always lies a cause for dread.'

"This world cannot another lady show,
If thou shouldst be untrue (as God defend),
Who would be cast in deeper depths of woe,
Than I, who shall be true unto the end;

Should any fate like that on me descend,
I could not live, and till just cause you find,
I pray to God, be not to me unkind!"

"BY ALL the Gods," cried Troilus, "above,
And all that dwell below this solid earth,
I've never swerved an instant in my love
From that first moment when it had its birth,
Nor ever shall I hold thee at less worth;
I can but say, to you I'm ever bound,
And truth thereof will in the end be found."

"Have all my thanks," she said, "O sweetheart mine,
And blessed Venus, ere I end my days,
Fulfil in Cressida thy great design,
And quit him well who merits all my praise!
As long as soul with living body stays,
I shall so strive, so true you've ever been,
That love with lasting honor we shall win.

"Believe me well that neither vain delight,
Nor royal rank, nor yet the high respect
Of you in war, or in the tourney fight,
Nor pomp, nor wealth, nor dress, did aught affect
My heart, and thy sole image there erect—
No, moral virtue, firmly set and true,
That was the reason why I first loved you.

"The gentle heart and manhood that you had,
And nobly cherished, ever in despite
Of all things leaning to the low and bad,
All coarseness and all vulgar appetite,
So that your reason bridled your delight—
For this I was above all others yours,
And shall be so, as long as life endures.

"Through length of years my love I'll not forsake,
Nor Fortune, mutable, shall e'er deface
My heart! But Jupiter, who well can make
The wretched glad, give us the happy grace
To meet again in ten nights in this place;
But now, alas, how swift the hour flies!
Farewell, dear heart, for now you must arise."

'TIS thus they end their long lamentings sad,
And kiss, and each in other's arms enfold;
But daylight breaks, and Troilus now clad,
Full sadly doth his lady's face behold,
As one who feels the breath of death so cold,
And with a grief that heavy on him bore,
Of last goodbyes he said to her a score.

I doubt if any head imagine can,
Or judgment weigh, or any tongue could tell
The cruel anguish of this woful man,
Surpassing all the torments dire of hell;
Since with his lady he no more may dwell,
His heart perturbed and dark with dread portent,
Forth from her chamber, silently he went.

BOOK V–
THE BETRAYAL

THE BETRAYAL

THE end approacheth of the destiny
Which Jove so long hath had in preparation,
And you, O Parcae, angry sisters three,
He trusteth with the fatal consummation!
Now Cressida must suffer love's probation,
And Troilus to grief himself resign
Which Lachesis his thread of life shall twine.

The gold-crowned Phoebus, high in heaven aloft,
Three times upon the earth below had seen
The molten snows, and Zephyrus as oft
Had brought again the tender leaflets green,
Since first the son of Hecuba the queen,
Began to cherish her for whom this sorrow
Had come, that she must leave him on the morrow.

Before the hour of nine came Diomede,
With him now Cressida from Troy must go;
The sorrows of her suffering heart exceed
All sorrow she had ever thought to know;
Yet all this inner grief she may not show,
But forth from out the Trojan town must fare,
And all the weight of woe in silence bear.

And Troilus, a lost and wandering sprite,
From whose sad heart all happiness was fled,
Had thoughts but of his lady fair and bright,
Who now, as ever, was the fountain-head
Of all his hope, the cure for all his dread.
But Troilus, farewell to hope of joy,
For thou shalt never see her back in Troy!

And since he could do nothing now but wait,
Full manfully he strove his grief to hide

From curious eyes, and at the city gate,
Whence forth upon her journey she should ride,
He and her friends to do her honor bide,
Though on his horse his seat he scarcely kept,
For grief unknown, unspoken and unwept.

What anger at his heart began to gnaw
When Diomede upon his steed drew near!
But anger now must yield to higher law,
Checked by his promised pledge, though not by fear.
"Alas," he sighed, "that I stand idle here!
Were it not better death should end this anguish,
Than evermore in lonely grief to languish?

"Why do I not the world and all defy,
And put a stop to this so hateful deed?
Why do I not all Trojan power deny?
Why do I not destroy this Diomede,
And carry her away upon my steed?
Why do I this misfortune so endure?
Why do I not risk all for my own cure?"

But there was reason why he could not do
These things, and must them sadly all resign;
For in his heart the fear of danger grew,
Not to himself, but fear lest any sign
Of violence should make the Greeks combine,
And in the wild disorder of the fray,
His helpless lady they in wrath would slay.

NOW Cressida is ready forth to ride,
Though far more gladly she would stay than go;
But to the Greeks she must, whate'er betide,
And to the world a willing face must show;
Thus forth she paces, statelily and slow,
And who can wonder that her heart should grieve,
Since all her love and joy she now must leave!

And Troilus, by way of courtesy,
With hawk on hand, and with an escort strong
Of knights, this lady doth accompany;
Across the valley rode the noble throng,
And even farther Troilus did long
To ride, but though it grieved him to do so,
Return he must, he may no farther go.

For at that moment forth Antenor came
From out the Grecian host, and those of Troy
Rejoiced and greeted him with loud acclaim;
And Troilus, though sharing not their joy,
Took heed restraining caution to employ,
And let no sign of sorrow mar his face,
But met Antenor with a kind embrace.

Such greetings made, his leave he now must take;
On Cressida he cast his lingering eye,
And to her side his way doth sadly make,
And took her hand to say a last goodbye,
While she, alas, doth naught but weep and sigh;
One word he softly said beneath his breath,
"Now hold your day, on that hangs life and death!"

His courser then he wheeled and rode away,
With face all pale, and unto Diomede
No word did he or any Trojan say,
Of which the son of Tydeus took heed,
Who knew a thing or two not in the Creed;
He took the lady's bridle at his side,
While back to Troy lone Troilus must ride.

NOW Diomede, who held her horse's bridle,
When all the folk of Troy had gone away,
Reflected, "All my labor shan't be idle,
If I have anything in this to say;
'Twill help at least at putting in the day.
I've heard it said, and read it in a book,
'He is a fool who doth himself o'erlook.'"

But Diomede was wise, with wit enough,
And mused, "I shall, I'm sure, accomplish naught
If I begin too soon, or treat her rough;
For if that man is dwelling in her thought
Whom I suppose, so soon he can't be brought
Out of her mind; but I shall find a way,
So she shan't guess what game I mean to play."

Then Diomede, attending at her side,
Remarked to her, she seemed a trifle sad,
And hoped she would not weary of the ride,
And anything she wanted, he'd be glad

To get for her, and do whate'er she bade,
For he was hers to order and command,
Till at her father's tent-door she should stand.

He swore upon his honor as a knight,
That nothing in the world would him more please,
Than to exert himself with will and might
To add unto her pleasure and her ease,
And hoped she would grow gladder by degrees,
"Because," he said, "we Greeks will all enjoy
Your company as much as those of Troy.

"Just now," he said, "you feel a little strange—
No wonder, since it's all so fresh and new,
From Trojan friends to Grecian friends to change,
Who all as yet are quite unknown to you;
But take my word for it, that just as true
A Greek you shall among our people find
As any Trojan, and just as well inclined.

"And since your friend I'll be, forever steady,
As I have sworn, to help you all I can,
And since we're old acquaintances already,
And since you know me best of any man,—
I mean of course among the Grecian clan—,
I hope that you will always feel quite free,
In case of any need, to call on me.

"Regard me as your brother, let me pray,
And take my friendship kindly, as 'tis meant;
And if perhaps some griefs upon you weigh,
I know not why, but all my heart is bent
On aiding you, if you will but consent;
And if your troubles deep I can't amend,
For sympathy at least on me depend.

"You Trojans towards us Greeks are filled with hate,
But so in every case it need not be;
For Greeks and Trojans likewise venerate
The God of Love as their divinity.
Hate whom you will, but be not wroth with me,
For no man living, you may well believe,
If you were angry, would more deeply grieve.

"But now we're drawing near your father's tent,
Whose eyes, I have no doubt, are turned this way;
With what I've said, I now must be content,
And leave the rest until some other day.
Give me your hand! I am, and shall be aye,
So heaven help me, while my life shall last,
In friendship yours, forever firm and fast.

"Such words to woman never have I spoken,
For by my hope of earthly happiness,
No woman have I given any token
Of love, and shall hereafter give still less,
If with your friendship, you my soul will bless;
Forgive me if my thought I rudely blurt,
For in these matters I am not expert.

"And do not be surprised, my lady bright,
That thus I speak to you of love so soon;
For I have heard of many a noble knight
Who, sight unseen, hath sought the lover's boon;
Nor have I power in me to oppugn
The God of Love, but must his will obey,
And ever shall, and for your mercy pray.

"There are such knights, so worthy, in this place,
And you so fair, that they will one and all
Bestir themselves to stand high in your grace;
But if such fortune to my lot should fall,
That me your humble servant you will call,
I promise here that I will serve as true
And faithfully as any man can do."

THIS blarney Cressida but vaguely heard,
So grievously at heart she was oppressed,
Although she could not help but catch a word
Or two, which she thought briefly it were best
To answer, letting so the matter rest;
But when at last her father came in sight,
Down from her horse she almost slipped from fright.

But still she spoke her thanks to Diomede
For all his trouble and his kindly care,
And for his profferred friendship, which indeed

She now accepted with a gracious air,
And hoped they'd meet again sometime somewhere,
And said she thought he was a trusty knight,
And down from off her horse did then alight.

Within his arms her father hath her taken,
And twenty times he kissed his daughter sweet.
"Welcome," he cried, "O daughter mine forsaken!"
And she, she said, was glad that they should meet
Again, and stood, submissive and discreet.
And here I leave her, her new life to lead,
For back to Troilus I now must speed.

TO TROY this woful Troilus returned,
Sorrow of sorrows now his hapless lot;
With angry brow all dallying he spurned,
But down from his horse without delay he got,
And to his chamber hastened like a shot;
His comrades were afraid a word to say,
For he did slight attention to them pay.

To all the woes that he so long had checked,
He had at last a chance to give free rein;
He cursed the Gods for all his hopes thus wrecked,
Jove and Apollo and Cupid, time and again,
Ceres, Bacchus and Venus, with might and main,
His birth, himself, his fate, the world so blind,
And save his lady, all of human kind.

To bed he goes, and tosses there and turns,
As does Ixion, suffering deep in hell,
And through the sleepless night he there sojurns;
But then his heart a little doth unswell,
Relieved by floods of tears that upward well;
His lady he began now to invoke,
And to himself these sorrowing words he spoke:

"O where is now my lovely lady dear?
Where are her breasts so white, O where, O where?
Where are her arms and where her eyes so clear,
Which yesternight were solace to my care?
Now I must weep alone in dark despair,
And blindly grope, but nothing in this place,
Except a pillow, find I to embrace!

"What shall I do? When will she come again?
God knows, alas! Why did I let her go?
O, would that I had perished there and then!
O precious heart, O Cressida, sweet foe,
O lady mine, my weeping eyes o'erflow!
With all my life and soul I thee endow,
But though I die, you can not aid me now!

"Who looks upon you now, my bright lodestar?
Who maketh now to thee his compliments?
Who comforts you, away from me so far?
Now I am gone, whom give you audience?
Who troubleth now to speak in my defence?
Alas, no man! And though I grieve and pine,
As evil is your fortune as is mine!

"And how shall I for ten whole days survive,
If I the first night suffer all this pain?
And how shall she, my sweetheart, keep alive?
How shall her tender heart such woe sustain?
What sorry signs of grief must still remain
Imprinted on her fair and gracious face
Until time brings her back unto this place!"

AND if he fell in any slumbering,
He did not cease to toss about and groan,
Or dream perhaps of some most dreadful thing,
As thus, that he must lie and ever moan,
Abandoned in some frightful place alone,
Or that he was among his foes withal,
And in their cruel hands about to fall.

And then convulsively he up would start,
And with the shock would suddenly awake,
While such a tremor ran throughout his heart,
The fear of it made all his body quake,
And horrid gasping sounds his breath would make,
For so it seemed, he fell from some high place,
Down to the lowest depths of endless space.

Upon his wretched state when he took thought,
His grief was greater than he well could bear,
But then he took himself in hand, and sought
To brighten up, and said he borrowed care,

And causeless was his grief and his despair,
Yet such devices brought but respite brief,
And hope soon yielded way to fear and grief.

O, who could all his woe relate,
His long-enduring sorrow and his pain?
Not all the men on earth incorporate!
Thus, reader, you will see why I refrain
To carry to its end this plaintive strain,
For how may this by my weak art be phrased,
When at the simple thought I stand amazed?

THE stars still lingered in the morning sky,
But the horizon eastward glimmered gray,
And pale and thin the moon had climbed on high—
In short the dawn came in its usual way,
And Phoebus, ushering in the rosy day,
Brightened the eastern sky as up he went,
And Troilus for faithful Pandar sent.

Now Pandar, all the livelong day before,
Had found no chance to proffer sympathy,
Although he knew his friend was suffering sore,
Because all day about the court he had to be,
But now at his first moment's liberty,
He quickly came, responsive to command,
Prepared by his afflicted friend to stand.

For in his heart he readily could guess
How Troilus, awake all night, would look,
And how he longed his sorrows to confess—
He knew this well enough without the book!
So to his chamber straight his way he took,
And there most somberly his friend he greeted
And by him on his bed himself he seated.

"My Pandar," then said Troilus, "the sorrow
Within my heart I may no more endure;
Today will be my last—, or else tomorrow—,
And of some final things I would make sure,
And most about my formal sepulture;
And will you please dispose of my estate,
As your good judgment may to you dictate.

"And of the fire and all the funeral flames,
To which my lifeless body thou shalt feed,
And of the feast and the palaestral games
To celebrate my wake, I pray take heed
That they be good; and offer Mars my steed,
My sword, my helmet, and, O brother dear,
My shield to Pallas give, the bright and clear.

"The powdered ash to which my heart shall burn,
I pray thee take and let it be confined
Within the vessel which men call an urn,
One made of gold, which then shall be consigned
To my fair lady, thus to keep in mind
My love and death, and bid my lady dear
Preserve it as a final souvenir.

"For now I feel approach the mortal throes,
And by my dreams, both old and new, I know
My time on earth is drawing near its close;
Besides the boding owl, Ascaphilo,
Two nights hath shrieked for me, the third I go!
To thee, O Mercury, I now confide
My wandering soul, to be its final guide."

TO THIS speech Pandar answered, "Troilus,
Dear friend, as I have told you oft before,
'Tis folly so, and most egregious,
To grieve, and now of this I'll say no more;
For he who heeds advice nor other lore,
He may for all that I shall say or do,
Alone in his own juice forever stew.

"But Troilus, I pray thee, tell me now,
Do you believe that any such delight
In love a living man hath known as thou?
Why, yes, God knows! And many a worthy wight
Has lacked his lady for a whole fortnight,
And hath not made one half the stir and fuss!
Why must you then be so tempestuous?

"For you yourself, on any day, may see,
How one must leave his lady-love or wife,
Through some compulsion or necessity,

Though she were dear to him as his own life,
Yet will not make such great to-do and strife;
For one takes such things as one takes the weather,
The best of friends can't always be together.

"And think upon the chaps whose loves are married
By force to other men, as happens oft,
And to a watchful husband's house are carried!
Hard hit such lovers are, but take it soft,
For hope survives to hold their hearts aloft;
Their needful time of sorrow they endure,
For time brings sorrow, and brings sorrow's cure.

"So take things as they come and let time slide,
And cultivate a joyous heart and light!
Ten days is not so long a time to bide.
For her return she pledged her honor bright,
And I am sure that she will come all right;
You need not fear but she will find a way,
I'm quite prepared my life on that to lay.

"And all your dreams and other such like folly,
To deep oblivion let them be consigned;
For they arise but from your melancholy,
By which your health is being undermined.
A straw for all the meaning you can find
In dreams! They aren't worth a hill of beans,
For no one knows what dreaming really means.

"Priests in the temples sometimes choose to say
That dreams come from the Gods as revelations;
But other times they speak another way,
And call them hellish false hallucinations!
And doctors say they come from complications,
Or fast or surfeit, or any other lie,
For who knows truly what they signify?

"And others say that through impressions deep,
As when one has a purpose firm in mind,
There come these visions in one's sleep;
And others say that they in old books find,
That every season hath its special kind
Of dream, and all depends upon the moon;
But all such folk are crazy as a loon!

"Dreams are the proper business of old wives,
Who draw their auguries from birds and fowls,
For which men often fear to lose their lives,
The raven's croak or mournful shriek of owls!
O why put trust in bestial shrieks and howls!
Alas, that noble man should be so brash
To implicate his mind in such like trash!

"And so with all my heart I thee beseech,
Against these melancholy thoughts to strive;
And pray get up, I've ended now my speech,
And let us plan something to help us drive
Dull care away, and keep us both alive
Till she returns, which won't be very long;
To waste the time in moping is all wrong.

"Come, let us think of those good times in Troy
That we have had, to pass the time away;
And think, besides, of those we shall enjoy
At some not very distant happy day.
These twice five days we'll fill with sport and play,
And so amuse ourselves with many things
That time will fly on self-oblivious wings.

"This town is full of nobles here and there,
The truce will last, besides, for yet some while,
I say, let's straightway to Sarpedon fare,
The distance to his house is but a mile;
And there we can the time at ease beguile,
Until there rolls around that happy morrow
When she returns, whose absence is thy sorrow.

"Get up then, friend and brother Troilus,
For truly it is scarcely worthy thee,
Upon thy bed to weep and cower thus;
For one thing certain you can take from me,
If thus you lie a day or two or three,
The folk will say you have a coward's heart,
And but for fear you play the sick man's part."

"O BROTHER dear," said Troilus replied,
"They know, whose heavy hearts have suffered pain,
When times of grief and sorrow shall betide
And deep affliction burns in every vein,

Then one cannot from cries of grief abstain;
And though I wept forever, I have good right,
For I have lost the source of all delight.

"But since I have to get up in the end,
I shall do so without too great delay,
And meantime pray that God will kindly send
As quickly as he can the glad tenth day!
For never was there bird as fain of May,
As I shall be when she comes back to Troy
Who causes all my grief as well as joy.

"But where do you suggest that we should go,
And where can we ourselves the best amuse?"
"My counsel is," said Pandar, "as you know,
To let Sarpedon counteract your blues."
After exchange of arguments and views,
Troilus at last thereto gave his assent,
And forth to good Sarpedon's house they went.

SARPEDON was a man in arms most able,
And famed throughout all Troy for living high;
And every costly dainty for the table
For daily entertainment he would buy,
And nothing to his guests he would deny,
Who always said, the greatest and the least,
They never had sat down to such a feast.

And in this world there was no instrument,
Sweet with the blast of air or touch of chord,
That skill of man could anywhere invent
For sounds that pleasure to the ear afford,
But it was heard around his festal board;
And ladies, too, to dance at his command
Were there, and ne'er was seen so fair a band.

But what avails all this to Troilus,
Whose inward grief absorbs his every thought
And rules his heart with will imperious!
His lady's memory he ever sought,
And longing such imagination wrought
Of this and that, his mind was never free
To take delight in this festivity.

The ladies, too, in throngs assembled there,
Since his was not among the number gay,
Gave him no ease of heart, though all were fair;
And on sweet instruments to hear men play,
While she was absent who hath borne away
The key of his heart, to him seemed blasphemy,
And vain abuse of such sweet melody.

Nor was there hour of all the day or night
When he said not, though not to listening ear,
"O Cressida, my lovely lady bright,
How have you fared since you have not been here?
O welcome back, my precious lady dear!"
Vain words were these, except his breath to cool,
For he was doomed to be but fortune's fool!

And all the letters old that she had sent
To him, he read them when he was alone,
And all the morning period thus he spent,
And in his fancy now her beauty shone
Afresh, and in his mind he caught the tone
Of her dear voice; four days he managed so,
And then resolved back home at once to go.

"Pandar," said he, "what are you thinking about?
Do you intend to keep on staying here,
Until Sarpedon tells us to get out?
I'm sure 'twill more considerate appear
For us to go; and now as eve draws near,
Let's say goodbye, and homeward let us turn,
For I just cannot longer here sojourn."

"Did we come here," said Pandar, "fetching fire,
To turn and run straight home with it again?
What better place than this can you desire?
We're with the most hospitable of men,
Sarpedon will but take it sadly when
We go, and your so hasty attitude
Would be, I think, unpardonably rude.

"Because we said that we had come to stay
A week with him, and now in so great haste
And on the fourth day thus to go away

Would hurt his feelings and be shocking taste;
He has himself at our disposal placed,
And since we've promised here a week to bide,
We should do so, and homeward then may ride."

Thus Pandar, both with force and argument,
Held him until the week had reached its end;
Sarpedon then they thanked and homeward went,
For Troilus would not his stay extend.
"Now God," he said, "this favor to me send,
That Cressida will be my welcoming,
When I get home," and so began to sing.

"Yes, in your eye," was what wise Pandar thought,
And to himself he said, quite soft and low,
"O, you'll cool off, my boy, if I know aught,
Ere Calchas lets his daughter from him go!"
But still of confidence he made a show,
And said that something told him in his heart
That she would come as soon as she could start.

And when at eve they reached the palace gate,
Down from their horses quickly they alight,
And to the room of Troilus go straight,
And sit them down and talk till almost night,
Which talk was all of Cressida the bright,
And afterward, when so they felt inclined,
They went to bed, though first of course they dined.

NEXT day, before the morning lights shone clear,
Troilus awoke, and leaping from his bed,
He routed Pandar out, his brother dear,
"For love of God," most plaintively he said,
"I cannot rest until I've visited
Her house, and though my eyes I cannot feast
On her, I can her palace see at least."

He found some way his household to mislead,
And he and Pandar to the town then go,
And to his lady's house at once proceed,
But, Lord, he only hastened to his woe!
He thought his heart with grief must overflow,
For when he saw the doors still bolted tight,
Upon his horse he scarce could sit upright.

For with one fatal glance his eyes behold
That shut is every window of the place,
And at the sight his heart like ice grows cold;
Without a word, and deadly pale of face,
Forth by the palace doth he madly race;
He spurs his horse and rides away full speed,
And of no man he takes the slightest heed.

"O palace desolate," he then began,
"O house, of houses once most dear to sight!
O palace, empty and accursed of man!
O lantern, wherein now is quenched the light!
O dwelling, once my day, now turned to night!
Why dost thou stand, while all my joys decay,
And she is gone, who was my hope and stay.

"O palace, once the crown of houses all,
Illumined with the sun of every bliss!
O ring, from which the ruby now doth fall!
O cause of woe, but cause of joy ere this!
Yet lacking better, fain now would I kiss
Thy doorways cold, if folk were not about!
Yet farewell, shrine, from which the saint is out!"

ON PANDAR then he cast his mournful eye,
With face all drawn and dreadful to behold,
And interrupted oft with many a sigh,
To him the devastating tale he told,
Of sorrow new and former joys grown old;
And pain sat on his countenance so grim,
No heart so hard but must have pitied him.

And then distraught, he rode there up and down,
And everything came back in memory
As he rode by the places in the town
In which he once had known felicity.
"Lo, yonder last I did her dancing see!
And in that temple by her eyes so clear,
First was I caught by my own lady dear!

"And yonder once I heard her laugh so bright,
And yonder once I saw her lightly play
And never since have seen so goodly sight!
And yonder once she came to me to say,

'O sweetheart mine, now love me well, I pray!'
And yonder such a loving glance she gave,
The thought of it will cheer me in my grave.

"And at that corner house upon this street,
I heard my most beloved lady dear,
With woman's voice so gentle and so sweet,
Singing withal so goodly and so clear
That in my soul methinks I yet can hear
The blissful sound! And in that yonder place
My dearest lady did I first embrace!

"O Cupid," then he thought, "O blessed Lord,
When all these things in memory I see,
How thou against me on all sides hast warred,
It seems just like a book of history!
But yet, why seek a conquest over me,
Since I am thine and wholly at thy will?
What joy has thou, thy subjects thus to kill?

"Thou hast, O Lord, avenged on me thy ire,
Thou God of might, and dangerous to grieve!
Have mercy, Lord! Thou knowest I desire
Nothing but thy good favor to receive;
Living and dying I shall in thee believe,
For all of which I beg a single boon,
That thou wilt send me Cressida back soon.

"Constrain her heart as quickly to return
As thou dost mine with longing her to see,
Then well I know she will not long sojourn.
Now, blessed Lord, show not such cruelty
Unto the blood of Troy, perilled in me,
As Juno showed unto the Theban race,
Nor let me perish here in lone disgrace!"

Forth to the city's open gates he rode,
Whence Cressida had started on her way,
And up and down there many a time he strode,
And often to himself "Alas!" did say,
"'Twas here I lost my bliss that fatal day,
And as she went, so may I have the joy
To see her now come riding back to Troy.

"As far as yonder hill, I was her guide,
And there I took of her my final leave,
And there I saw her to her father ride,
The thought of which my heart in two will cleave;
And hither came I home when it was eve,
And here bereft of every joy I dwell,
And must so bide till time makes all things well."

SICK in his fancy, he imagined oft
That he was looking gaunt and pale and thin,
And that men noticed it and whispered soft,
"What can it be? What trouble is he in?
It must be bad, because he looks like sin!"
But this was all by melancholy bred,
Which spun such foolish fancies in his head.

At other times, in his fantastic brain,
He thought that every man along the way
Gave him such pitying looks as said quite plain,
"Poor Troilus, he's nearing his last day!"
'Twas so he passed his time in sad dismay,
And in these troubled days his life he led,
Still wavering in mind twixt hope and dread.

Some little joy he took in song to show
The reason for his grief, as best he might,
For heavy hearts when they in words o'erflow,
By such discharge may sometimes grow more light;
And so, when he was out of all men's sight,
With gentle voice unto his lady dear,
Though absent, yet he sang as you shall hear:

"O star, now I have lost thy cheering light,
With grief unending may I well bewail,
That in dark torment ever night by night
Toward certain death with favoring wind I sail!
And if the sacred tenth night there should fail
Thy beams to guide me through that fatal hour,
Charybdis shall my ship and me devour!"

WHEN he had sung his song, thereafter soon
He fell again into his sighings old,
And every night he gazed upon the moon,

Shining with light so clear, but pale and cold,
And all his sorrow to the moon he told,
And said, "When thy two horns again are new,
I shall be glad, if all the world holds true.

"Thy horns were old upon that luckless morrow
When from this place rode forth my lady dear,
The cause of all my torment and my sorrow.
And O Lucina, bright and ever clear,
Run fast, I beg, about thy circling sphere,
For when thy horns anew begin to spring,
To Troy again my lady shall they bring."

The days stretched out, and longer every night
Seemed to this mind increasingly to grow,
And that the sun ran on his course unright,
By longer way than it was wont to go.
"In truth," he said, "I fear it must be so,
That Phaeton, son of the sun, alive,
Doth still amiss his father's chariot drive!"

And on the city's walls he oft would walk,
And gaze where he could see the Grecian host,
And to himself in this wise would he talk,
"Lo, yonder lies the one I love the most!
Lo, yonder the tent whence like a pining ghost,
There comes this sighing breeze so gently blowing,
New life upon my lifeless soul bestowing.

"And verily this wind, that more and more
Increases steadily upon my face,
Is from my lady's sighs, so deep and sore;
In proof of which, there is no other space
Of all this town, but only in this place
I feel a wind that soundeth so like pain;
It saith, 'Alas, why parted are we twain!'"

The tedious time he passes in this way
And thus survives until the last ninth night;
And Pandar still was his support and stay,
Striving with all his patience and his might
To cheer his friend and make his heart more light,
Feeding his hope that on the tenth tomorrow,
Cressida would come again and end his sorrow.

NOW Cressida, upon the other side,
In exile lone among the Greeks must dwell,
And many a time a day, "Alas," she cried,
"That I was born! My wretched heart may well
Long for the tolling of my burial bell!
Alas, that fortune such hostility
Should single out to show to harmless me!

"My father will not grant me my request,
For anything that I can do or say,
And Troilus as treason self-confessed
Will take it, if too long from Troy I stay,
Nor could he see it any other way!
Thus shall I have the worst on every side,
Alas, that such fate should to me betide.

"And if the risky project I should try,
To steal away by night, then were I caught,
I should be taken surely for a spy;
Or else, indeed a still more dreadful thought,
Into some ruffian's hands I might be brought.
So am I lost, whichever way I turn,
Nor find the peace for which my heart doth yearn!"

Now pale and wan had grown her lovely face,
Her body, too, with grief doth waste away;
From dawn to night she gazed upon the place,
Which was her home for many a happy day,
And all the sleepless night she weeping lay;
No remedy she knew for all her care,
And day and night were sunk in black despair.

In all this time she found her greatest ease
In keeping in her heart the image bright
Of Troilus, and his fair qualities
And all his goodly words she would recite
Since first she took him for her loving knight,
Cherishing in her woful heart the fires
Of love by such fond thoughts as love inspires.

In all this world so wide, no heart of stone
But must have melted at her grievous sorrow,
As there she wept abandoned and alone;
At thought of Troilus at eve and morrow,

She had no need of others' tears to borrow,
And this was yet the worst of all her grief,
That she could tell no one for her relief.

With sad and mournful eyes she looked on Troy,
On every tower high and every hall.
"Alas," she said, "the pleasure and the joy
Which I have known within that city wall,
But now all turned to bitterness and gall!
O Troilus, what art thou doing now?
Art thou still faithful to thy lover's vow?

"Would I had done as you did once require,
Had fled with you to some security,
Then would I not in lonely grief expire!
That it was right, O who would not agree
With such a one as Troilus to flee;
But when the corpse is ready to put in
The grave, too late to think of medicine!

"Too late, too late, the evil to repair!
Prudence, alas, one of thy triple eyes
I lacked in management of this affair!
Of time long past I was aware and wise,
And present things could at their value prize,
But future time, ere I was fairly caught,
I could not see, and so thus low am brought.

"But now I say, betide what may betide,
I shall tomorrow night, by hook or crook,
Steal from this camp, and when I get outside,
With Troilus I'll seek some happy nook
Where we can dwell; I care not how men look
At it, or how the gossips' tongues may wag,
True love they always in the mire will drag.

"If every gossip's word you were to heed,
Or rule yourself by other people's wit,
'Twould be a pretty life that you would lead;
Whate'er you do, some will find fault with it,
Yet others think it proper, right and fit;
And in such matters of dubiety,
My happiness will compensate for me.

"I know, then, now at last, what I shall do,
I'll go to Troy, and thus the matter end!"
But time would come, and ere a month or two,
When quite another way her mind would tend!
Troilus and Troy together she would send
Their way, quite readily would let them slide,
And happily among the Greeks abide.

NOW Diomede, of whom I spoke before,
Hath still his mind intent upon one thing,
Which in his inmost heart he ever bore,
How he with some device encompassing,
Cressida's heart into his net might bring.
To catch this lady was his sole design,
And to this end he laid out hook and line.

But he was wary, since he surely thought
That she had left some love in Troy behind,
For ever since she from that town was brought,
She seemed to carry something on her mind,
Some loss to which she could not be resigned.
"But still," he said, "to try is worth the pains,
For he who nothing ventures, nothing gains."

And so he said unto himself one day,
"Now I am not a fool! I see well how
She's sad because her lover is away;
If I should be too brisk with her just now,
It wouldn't do; I must some time allow;
Wise folk in books this matter thus express,
'Do not make love to those in great distress.'

"But such a flower for yourself to win
From him for whom she mourneth night and day,
That were a conquest one might glory in!"
And boldly then, for he loved not delay,
"Let happen," he declared, "whatever may,
I'll try her out, and if she should refuse,
I've nothing but a little breath to lose."

THIS Diomede, as all the books attest,
Was quick in action, also brave and bold,
And stern of voice, with mighty arms and chest;

For feats adventurous he was extolled,
High as his father Tydeus of old;
Some say his word could not be counted on,
This prince of Argos and of Calydon.

Cressida was in frame of even height,
And in her shape, her look and all her face,
No fairer creature ever blessed man's sight,
Following the custom of her time and place,
She wore her hair all braided in a lace,
Down by her collar at her back behind,
And with a thread of gold she did it bind.

Her curving brows beneath her forehead met,
And in all things men counted her most fair;
Her eyes within their frame were brightly set,
And all who saw her with one voice declare
That Paradise in truth was written there;
Beauty and love in her were so create,
That which the greater, one could but debate.

Sedate she was, simple and wise withal,
Instructed in the arts most carefully,
Goodly of speech, whatever might befall,
With kindly grace, but dignified and free;
Nor lacked her heart in sensibility
In all the things which sympathy engage,
But I regret I cannot tell her age.

And Troilus was more than middle height,
But well-proportioned and of figure neat;
In short, he seemed in everything just right,
Young, fresh, and quick as a lion on his feet,
And true as steel his heart within its seat;
He was with all the qualities endowed,
That to our human nature are allowed.

In all the histories it is related
That Troilus was never in men's sight
In lower rank than with the highest rated,
In noble deeds pertaining to a knight;
Though not a giant in his body's might,
His heart was ever equal to the best,
In deeds that knightly competence attest.

BUT now let us return to Diomede.
The tenth day came since that sad parting day
When to the Greeks this lady he did lead,
And Diomede, fresh as the flowers in May,
Came to the tent where wise old Calchas lay,
And feigned that he had business with the priest,
But of his plans, the business was the least.

Now Cressida, in all things neat and nice,
Received him there, and bade him take a seat,
Nor had she any need to ask him twice;
And in the proper way a guest to treat,
Spices and wine she served in manner meet;
In friendly conversation then they fell,
A part of which I shall proceed to tell.

First of the war he then began to speak
Between the Greeks and the besieged in Troy,
And her opinion doth he humbly seek
What methods in the siege one should employ;
And then he asked her if she did enjoy
Her life among the Greeks, and if their ways
Seemed strange, and how she passed her days,

And why her father should delay so long
To marry her to some good worthy knight.
But Cressida, who felt the pain still strong
For absent Troilus, her heart's delight,
Gave answer to his questions as she might,
But of his deeper purpose and intent,
Perhaps she had no inkling what he meant.

But nevertheless the dauntless Diomede
Pressed bravely on, and this attempt essayed:
"If I have rightly of you taken heed
Dear Cressida, I'm very much afraid,
Since hand upon your bridle first I laid,
When you came forth from Troy upon that morrow,
You have been sore oppressed by some deep sorrow.

"I cannot say just what the cause may be,
Unless perhaps some Trojan you hold dear,
Yet let me say, it truly would grieve me
If you for any Trojan, far or near,

Should ever spill a quarter of a tear,
Or let one from your face drive off the smile,
For, Cressida, it isn't worth the while.

"The Trojans, one might say, both all and some,
Are prisoners, and never shall be free,
For out of Troy not one alive shall come,
For all the gold between the sun and sea;
You can take this for utter certainty,
No single one shall come from thence alive,
Although he were the lord of worlds twice five.

"The rape of Helen we shall so repay,
Ere we upon our homeward way shall wend,
The Manes, Gods of pain, shall be afraid
Lest Grecian wrath with theirs should e'er contend;
And men shall fear, until this world shall end,
Henceforth forever to abduct a queen,
Such vengeance on the Trojans shall be seen.

"For either Calchas tricks us with ambages,
That is, with words of double meaning sly,
Such as we call a word with two visages,
Or that I speak the truth, none can deny;
For all of this you'll see with your own eye,
And you shan't need to wait for many a moon,
Mind what I say, you'll be surprised how soon!

"Do you suppose your father, old and wise,
Would give Antenor for you in this war,
Unless he knew just how the matter lies,
And what fate for the Trojans is in store?
He knows full well that there is no hope for
A single Trojan, and so he didn't dare
To let you stay among them over there.

"What further can you ask, my lady dear?
Both Troy and Trojans from your heart erase!
Drive out this futile hope and make good cheer,
Restore again your beauty to its place,
Which with the salt of tears you now deface!
For Troy is brought at last to such a state,
To save her now, it is too late a date.

"Besides, you shall among us Grecians find
A love more perfect, and a truer knight
Than any Trojan is, and one more kind,
To honor you with all his strength and might;
If you will listen to me, lady bright,
Myself will be the man, and for the price,
A dozen Greeces I would sacrifice."

And with that word he blushed a bashful red,
And as he spoke, his voice trembled and shook,
The while he turned aside and bowed his head,
And paused, but soon new courage took,
And with a serious, but a gentle look,
He said, "I am, though this gives you no joy,
As good a gentleman as dwells in Troy.

"For if my father Tydeus," he said,
"Had longer lived, I would have been ere this
Of Calydon and Argos king and head,
And shall be yet, unless my guess I miss.
But he was slain, and lost all earthly bliss,
At Thebes, where Polynices and his men
Good reason had to grieve in sorrow then.

"But, lady dear, since now I am your man,
And in my heart you hold the chiefest place,
And I shall serve you every way I can,
As long as I exist in time and space,
So look upon me with a kindly face,
And grant that I may come again tomorrow
And tell you more at leisure of my sorrow."

WHY should I all his pretty speeches tell?
He spoke enough for one day, that is sure,
And what he said to her, he said so well,
That her consent at last he doth procure
To come again, though first she did adjure
Him not to raise the topic he had broached,
At which, no doubt, he felt himself reproached!

But still her heart was set on Troilus,
And his dear image she could not erase
From out her mind, and so she answered thus:

"O Diomede, I love that happy place
Where I was born! May heaven in its grace
Deliver it from out its sorry state
And grant to hapless Troy a happy fate!

"And that the Greeks on Troy their wrath would wreak,
I know that very well! But after all,
It may not happen as you say and speak,
And God forbid that such thing should befall;
I know my father did me to him call,
And that he dearly bought me, as you say,
And for all this, I shall him well repay!

"And that the Greeks are men of high renown,
I know that, too; but truly you shall find
As worthy folk within the Trojan town,
As able, too, as perfect and as kind,
As any twixt the Orcades and Ind.
And that some lady gladly would receive
Your service, that I'm ready to believe.

"But as for love," she said, and gently sighed,
"I had a lord, and I his wedded wife,
To whom my heart was pledged until he died;
But other love than that in all my life
There hath not been, nor shall I seek love's strife.
And that you are of high and noble birth,
That have I heard, and know you for your worth.

"And for that reason now I wonder,
That any woman you should trouble so!
For love and I are very far asunder,
And I am more inclined, as things now go,
To spend my life in mourning and in woe,
Though how my heart may change, I cannot tell;
The future may, of course, my grief dispel.

"But now I am afflicted and cast down,
And you in arms are busy day by day;
But later, when you Greeks have won the town,
There's just a chance that then it happen may,
If things turn out in unexpected way,
That I shall do what I ne'er thought to do,
And what I've said should be enough for you.

"Come back tomorrow, if you so desire,
But do not push this matter now too far.
Come when you want, if that's all you require!
But ere you go, at least I'll say, you are,
So help me Pallas, gleaming like a star,
The one of all within the Grecian city
Who first could rouse my heart to throbs of pity.

"I do not say I promise what you seek,
Nor yet deny. So do not fret nor frown,
For thou hast need to fear no other Greek!"
Pausing at these concessions, she looked down
And deeply sighing said, "O Trojan town,
Pray God that thou shalt be in safety first,
Or else my wretched heart in grief shall burst!"

But Diomede was not all dismayed,
And broughts forth arguments all fresh and new,
And with insistence for her favor prayed,
And thereupon, the most that he could do,
He took her glove, and called it love-pledge true,
And finally, when it drew on towards eve,
And all was well, he rose and took his leave.

BRIGHT Venus soon appeared to point the way
Where Phoebus, wide and round, should down alight,
And now her chariot horses Cynthia
Whirls out of the Lion, driven by her might,
And Signifer displays his candles bright;
Then Cressida unto her night-rest went
Within her father's fair and shining tent,

Debating in her soul aye up and down
The words of this impetuous Diomede,
His high estate, the peril of the town,
Her loneliness and all her pressing need
Of friendly help, and thus began to breed
The reasons why, the simple truth to tell,
She thought it best among the Greeks to dwell.

The morrow came, and like a confessor
Came Diomede, who cunningly displayed
His arguments and added many more,
And such an all-persuasive case he made,

That her misgivings were almost allayed,
And finally, to state the matter plain,
She found in him a surcease from her pain.

And afterward, the story telleth us,
She gave him back the bay, the noble steed
Which once he won from hapless Troilus;
A brooch besides—and that was little need—
Her lover's gift, she gave to Diomede,
And as her knight she doth him now receive,
And made for him a pennant of her sleeve.

And elsewhere in the story it is told,
When deeply wounded once was Diomede,
By Troilus, she wept tears manifold
When she beheld his wide wounds freshly bleed,
And in the care of him she took great heed,
And then, to heal his wound in every part,
Men say, men say she gave to him her heart.

And yet the story also telleth us,
No woman ever did so deep lament
For love betrayed as she for Troilus!
"Alas," she cried, "forever lost and spent
Is all my truth in love's high sacrament!
The gentlest man, the noblest ever made
Have I in falsehood wilfully betrayed!

"Alas, of me unto the world's last end,
There shall be neither written nor yet sung
A kindly word! No one will me defend!
O rolled shall be my name on many a tongue,
Throughout the world my bell shall wide be rung,
And women will despise me most of all!
Alas, that such a fate on me should fall!

"And they will say, in scorning of all this,
That I dishonored them, alack the day;
Though I were not the first that did amiss,
That will not wipe the blot of shame away!
But since what's done, must so forever stay,
And since my former guilt I can't undo.
To Diomede at least I shall be true.

"But Troilus, since I can do no more,
And since our paths henceforth must separate,
May heaven to its favor thee restore!
O Troilus, the best and gentlest mate
Who e'er his heart to love did consecrate,
What other love can stand in thy dear stead!"
She broke down then, and bitter tears she shed.

"Of this I'm sure, that I shall hate you never,
A friend's love you shall have at least of me,
And my good word, though I should live forever!
And truly I should grieve if I should see
You ever fall into adversity.
That you are guiltless, no one need me tell!
God's will be done! And thus I say farewell!"

HOW long a time it was that lay between
Ere she forsook him for bold Diomede,
No author tells, so far as I have seen,
And no man, let him ne'er so widely read,
Shall find a further record of this deed;
But Diomede, though quick enough to woo,
Before he won her, had yet more to do.

Nor shall I now this woman further chide
Than from her simple story doth arise;
Her name, alas, is published far and wide,
Her guilt is plain enough to all men's eyes;
And if I could condone in any wise
Her deed, in pity's name I would assent,
For of her sin she did at least repent.

POOR Troilus, as I before have told,
Now lived along in any way he might,
But often was his heart now hot, now cold,
And most of all upon that last ninth night,
For still he hoped next day his lady bright
Would come again; but yet he had, God knows,
Throughout that wakeful night but slight repose.

Phoebus, the laurel-crowned, now shiningly
Upon his course aye higher upward went
To warm the wide waves of the eastern sea,

And Nisus' daughter sang the day's advent,
When Troilus his word for Pandar sent,
And on the city walls they walked about,
To keep for Cressida a far lookout.

Till noon they kept their place and looked to see
Who came, and every one, they said, as long
As he was far away, was surely she,
Till nearer view showed they were always wrong,
For she was never one in any throng;
And thus befooled, this fond expectant pair
Stand on the Trojan walls and vainly stare.

Said Troilus, "Unless she comes quite soon,
I must believe she couldn't get away
And won't arrive in town till afternoon.
No doubt she had enough to do and say
To get from under her old father's sway.
I think, perhaps, he wanted her to dine
Before she left, and she could not decline."

Pandar to this replied, "That may well be,
And let us do the same, I might suggest,
And then come back, to see what we can see."
So home they go and dine and briefly rest,
Then back again upon their hopeless quest.
They cannot see, for all their straining eyes,
That fortune hides from them a sad surprise.

"It looks," said Troilus, "as though something
Has happened, or else her father keeps her so
She can't arrive till nearly evening.
Come on, and to the city gates let's go!
These gatemen are such stupid dolts, you know,
They wouldn't hesitate to shut the gate
And keep her out, if she chanced to be late."

The day goes fast, night falls on land and sea,
And "Cressida, she cometh not," he said.
He gazes forth on hedge and grove and tree,
And from the city wall he hangs his head,
But still she tarries, still his hopes he fed.
"I know," he cried, "what she intends to do!
Almost I feared that she would prove untrue!

"But now I know just what she doth intend—
She means to travel here incognito,
And her good sense therein I must commend.
She will not make herself a public show,
But quietly, and so that none may know,
By night into the town she means to ride,
And her good pleasure we must so abide.

"In fact there's nothing else that we can do.
But Pandar, look! What is it there I see?
She's come at last, it's too good to be true!
Lift up your eyes, old man! Is not that she?"
"Well, no," said Pandar, "sorry I can't agree!
You're wrong again, my boy, and for my part,
All I can see is some poor farmer's cart."

"Too true, it's but too true," said Troilus,
"But still I cannot think it's all for naught
That in my heart I feel uplifted thus.
Some good must be foreshadowed by my thought,
Since consolation comes to me unsought;
I never felt such comfort, truth to say,
And that she'll come tonight, my life I'll lay."

"It may be," answered Pandar, "well enough,"
Nor any of his empty hopes denied,
Though in his heart he thought it silly stuff,
And with straight face said to himself aside,
"You might as well give up and let things slide,
For all the good you'll get by waiting here.
Yes, farewell to the snows of yesteryear!"

THE warden of the gates began to call
The folk without the fosses to prepare
To drive into the town their cattle all,
Or through the night they must remain out there;
And in the dusk, with heart oppressed by care,
Troilus turns at last homeward to ride,
For now why should he longer there abide!

But still he took some hope in thinking this,
That he perhaps had counted wrong the day.
"I must," he said, "have taken her amiss,
For I recall I heard her that night say,

'I shall be back again, if so I may,
Before the silver moon, my own sweetheart,
Shall pass the Lion and from the Ram depart,'

"And so it may yet turn out for the best."
And on the morrow, to the gate he went,
And up and down, to east and then to west,
Beyond the city walls his gaze he bent,
But nothing gained from weary time thus spent,
And so at night, when he could see no more,
He went back home in disappointment sore.

NOW hope delusive took its final flight,
For all that he had sought had turned out wrong;
Upon his heart there fell a deadly blight,
So were his silent sorrows sharp and strong,
For when he saw she stayed away so long,
He dared not to himself or think or say
Why she should fail to keep her promised day.

The third, the fourth, the fifth, the sixth succeed,
Since the appointed ten days by had rolled,
And hope and dread still battle for the lead,
Nor could he quite reject her pledges old;
But then he saw her word she would not hold,
And this last woe completely filled his cup,
And he had nothing now to keep his courage up.

The dark and wicked mood of jealousy,
Which drives men on until they grow insane,
Crept in his heart to keep grief company,
And from all food and drink he did abstain,
As one who on this earth would not remain;
A lonely, melancholy life he led,
And from companionship he turned and fled.

A sick man now, his body's powers fail,
He seems a stranger even to his friends;
So thin and gaunt, of face so wan and pale,
Upon a staff he weakly now depends,
For thus black care achieves its evil ends;
And if one asked him how it all did start,
He said he had some trouble with his heart.

Priam inquired, and so his mother dear,
His brothers and his sisters, too, did ask,
Why he should always be so sad and drear,
And for his good they took him oft to task;
But still his grief he ever sought to mask,
And said about his heart he felt such pain
As mortal body could not long sustain.

IT CHANCED one day he laid him down to sleep,
And in his restless slumber, so he thought,
Within a wood he went to walk and weep,
For love of her who all this wrong had wrought,
And down a path, his eyes a vision caught;
A tusked boar appeared in his sad dreams,
Asleep and lying in the bright sunbeams,

And by this boar, whom in her arms she held,
Lay Cressida, kissing the fearsome beast.
And suddenly this vision strange expelled
All sleep, and from his dreaming thus released,
Troilus knew all hope for him had ceased.
"O Pandar," cried he, "now I know the worst!
I am a man abandoned and accursed!

"My lady Cressida hath me betrayed,
In whom was all my trust and my delight;
Her love she hath elsewhere conveyed!
The blessed Gods above through their great might
Have in my dreams revealed it to my sight!
Thus in my dreams I did my love behold—"
And all the tale to Pandar he then told.

"O Cressida, what baseless treachery,
What lust of heart, what beauty or what wit—,
What wrath with just cause have you felt towards me?
What guilt in me, what thoughts or deeds unfit
Have caused thy heart away from me to flit?
O trust! O faith! O hopes that life inspire!
O who hath robbed me of my heart's desire!

"Alas, why did I ever let you go?
O, by what folly was I thus misled?
What faith on oaths can I henceforth bestow!

God knows I was convinced in heart and head,
That every word was Gospel that you said.
But treason oft doth show its hateful face
In those in whom the greatest trust we place.

"What shall I do? What now is left for me?
There falls on me anew so sharp a pain,
For which there can be found no remedy,
Better to kill myself with these hands twain
Than in this life of misery remain!
Death at the least a final peace will send,
But life is daily death that hath no end!"

Then Pandar answered him, "Alas the while
That I was born! Have I not said ere this,
That dreams all sorts of folk all times beguile?
And why? They all interpret them amiss!
To charge her false on dreams is cowardice,
Because your dreams rise only from your fear,
And what they mean, you never can make clear.

"This dream that you have had about a boar,
It well may be that it doth signify
Her father, old and of his head so hoar,
Who near his death doth in the warm sun lie,
While she for natural grief must weep and cry,
And kiss him as he lies there on the ground—
This is the way you should your dream expound."

"Perhaps," said Troilus. "I wish I knew
For certain how to judge my dream aright."
"I'll tell you then," said Pandar, "what to do!
Since you know well enough how to endite,
Bestir yourself and to your lady write.
I know no better way of finding out
The truth and freeing so your mind of doubt.

"That way you'll know just how things stand, for better
Or worse; for if untrue she means to be,
She will not send an answer to your letter;
And if she writes, then you can quickly see
If she to come again to Troy is free,
And if she's let and hindered in some way,
She will explain it all as clear as day.

"You have not written her since forth she went,
Nor has she written you, and I dare say
Some little things her coming back prevent,
And when you know just what they are, you may
Decide she's acted in the wisest way.
Go then and write; of all plans that's the best
To ease your mind and set your doubts at rest."

Troilus to this advice can but agree,
For other plan he has none to propose,
Nor long delays, but sits down hastily,
Debating in his heart the cons and pros
How he may best portray to her his woes,
And thus to Cressida, his lady dear,
He wrote this letter as it follows here:

"FLOWER of my life, whom I do rightly call
Sole sovereign of my every act and deed,
With body and soul, with will and thought and all,
I, wretched man, answering every need
That tongue may tell or heart may ever plead,
As far as matter occupieth space,
I, wretched man, beseech of you your grace!

"And let me now recall, my own sweetheart,
How long a lonely time has passed away,
Since you left me, pierced with the bitter dart
Of pain, for which no help nor stay
Have I yet had, but ever worse from day
To day, and so must I forever dwell
Until you come my sorrow to dispel.

"With heart oppressed by fear, yet firm and true,
As one by need hard driven now I write,
And all my grief that ever grows anew,
With such skill as I have, I here endite,
And all these stains upon this parchment white
Are tears which from my eyes upon it rain,
And let them plead my sorrow not in vain!

"The first I beg is that with eyes so clear
You'll look at this, and hold it not defiled;
And yet again, that you, my lady dear,
Will read it with a gentle heart and mild.

And if my words should seem abrupt or wild,
Bethink that from my grief they all do start,
And so forgive them me, my own sweetheart.

"If any lover ever durst with right
Upon his lady chargefully complain,
Then surely I am that unlucky wight,
Considering how you have for these months twain
Delayed, although you said, time and again,
But ten days with the Greeks you would sojourn—
Yet in two months, you do not yet return.

"But since in all things I must to you yield,
I may say nothing further on this score,
Yet humbly and with sorrow unconcealed,
I here set forth all my affliction sore,
From day to day desiring ever more
To know in full how with the Greeks you fare,
And what you have been doing over there.

"Your health and fortune may the Lord increase,
And may your honor upward in degree
Advance, and in its growing never cease;
The hopes you cherish, every wish and plea,
The Gods grant them to you all utterly!
And may some pity thereamongst shine through
Towards me, thy faithful knight and ever true.

"And if you would know how in Troy I fare,
Whose griefs now at their pinnacle arrive,
I can but say, that borne upon by care,
The time I wrote this, I was yet alive,
Yet ready, too, with swift death to connive,
Which I hold off, and from me briefly fend,
Until I see what word to me you send.

"My eyes, now useless your fair face to see,
Of bitter tears are but two flowing wells,
My song is but of my adversity,
My happy heavens turn to bitter hells,
And no relief my weight of woe dispels;
I am my own accused adversary,
And every joy turns into its contrary.

"But when you come back home again to Troy,
All this affliction you may soon redress,
For then indeed you shall revive my joy,
For never yet did heaven a heart so bless
As you shall mine, when all my long distress
Shall come to end; if not by pity stirred,
Stern duty bids you hold at least your word.

"But if I've earned this fate by doing wrong,
Or if my face you ne'er again will see,
In mere reward that I have served you long,
I beg that you will be both frank and free,
And quickly write and send word back to me
And tell me so, my only lodestar bright,
That I may end my life in death and night.

"Or if some other cause makes you to dwell,
Then in your letter make of this report,
For though to me your absence is a hell,
My woe to needful patience can resort,
And hope against my black despair retort.
Pray write then, sweet, and make the matter plain,
With hope, or death, deliver me from pain!

"But I must warn you, my own sweetheart true,
When you again your Troilus shall see,
So much has changed his frame and all his hue,
That Cressida shall scarcely know it's he.
In truth, light of my world, my lady free,
So thirsts my heart your beauty to behold,
My grasp on life I scarce can longer hold.

"I say no more, though more I well could write,
And still leave boundless volumes yet to say;
With life or death my love you may requite,
Yet heaven grant you joy in every way!
So fare thee well, my love, and have a good day!
My life or death I take as you shall send
And to your truth myself I still commend,

"With such good will, that if you grant to me
The same good will, there's nothing else I crave;
For in you lies, if so you'll have it be,

The doom that men shall dig for me my grave,
 Or in you lies the might my life to save,
 And bid all grief and pain from me depart!
 And now a last farewell, my own sweetheart!

LE VOSTRE T."

TO CRESSIDA this letter straight was sent,
To which her answer was to this effect:
Her long delay she sadly did lament,
And said that she would come when good prospect
She found, and what was wrong would all correct,
And finally she wrote and told him then
That she would come, O yes, but knew not when.

But still her letter seemed most cordial,
Though in the end he found it vague and cold,
And yet she swore she loved him best of all!
But Troilus, when all the tale is told,
Cressida hath left thee here the bag to hold!
Thus goes the world! God shield us from disaster,
And of our fates may each of us be master!

THE grief of Troilus grew greater night
And day, so long his lady from him stayed,
And feebler grew his hope and body's might,
For which upon his bed himself he laid,
Nor ate, nor drank, nor slept, nor speech essayed,
And thought upon the curse of fortune blind,
Until all reason fled from out his mind.

This dream, of which I have already told,
He never from his fancy could expel,
Nor could he doubt his lady had grown cold,
Nor yet that Jove had taken means to tell
By dreams, when heavy sleep upon him fell,
Of her untruth and his disastrous fate—
All which the boar was meant to indicate.

Then for his sister Sibyl straight he sent,
Known also as Cassandra round about,
And told his dream to her just as it went,
And asked her to resolve his mind of doubt,
Concerning this great boar with tusks so stout;
And soon as she the meaning of it found,
She thus began his vision to expound.

Smiling a prophet's smile, "O brother dear,"
She said, "If you the truth will really know,
Then you must first a few old stories hear,
Which tell how fortune once did overthrow
Some lords of old, and thereby I shall show
And tell you whence this boar, and of what kind,
As in the books the story you may find.

"Diana, filled with anger and with ire,
Because the Greeks withheld her sacrifice,
Nor on her altar set incense afire,
In vengeance made them pay a cruel price,
And this, in long and short, was her device,
She let a boar, as great as ox in stall,
Devour their growing corn and vines and all.

"To slay this boar the countryside was raised,
And thereamong came one, the boar to see,
A maiden whom all in that region praised;
And Meleager, lord of that country,
So loved this maiden, fair and fresh and free,
That into battle with this boar he went,
And killing it, its head unto her sent.

"From this, as ancient writers tell to us,
There rose a contest and a warfare high,
And from this lord descended Tydeus,
By line direct, as no one can deny;
But how this Meleager came to die
Through his own mother, that I shall not tell,
For on that tale it were too long to dwell."

How Tydeus made warfare Sibyl told,
At Thebes, that ancient city and so strong,
Maintaining that to Polynices bold,
The Theban city did by right belong,
And that Eteocles, his brother, wrong
Had done, in holding Thebes by strength—
All this she told to him and at great length.

She also told about Haemonides,
When Tydeus slew fifty knights so stout,
And told of all the wondrous prophecies,
And how the seven kings for Thebes set out,

And then besieged the city round about,
And of the holy serpent and the well,
And of the Furies, all this did she tell;

And Archemorus' death and funeral plays,
And how Amphiorax fell through the ground,
How Tydeus was slain and closed his days,
And also how Ipomedon was drowned,
And Parthenope final death wound found,
And how Capaneus, the strong and proud,
Was slain by stroke of thunder, sounding loud.

And then she told the tale how either brother,
Eteocles and Polynices true,
How each of them in skirmish killed the other,
And how Argia wept and made ado;
The burning of the town did she review,
And so descended down from stories old
To Diomede, and of him thus she told.

"This boar you dreamed of stands for Diomede,
Tydeus' son, of Meleager's line,
Who killed the boar and won fame by that deed;
Thy lady, if in fact she once was thine,
With Diomede in love doth now combine;
Be glad or sad, but there can be no doubt,
This Diomede is in and you are out."

"That isn't true," he cried, "thou sorceress!
False is the spirit of thy prophecy,
And all the priestly cunning you profess!
Your wickedness is plain and clear to see,
To stain a lady's name with falsity!
Away," he cried, "may Jove increase your sorrow,
For you are false today and false tomorrow!

"As well defame the beautiful Alceste,
Who was, unless all history doth lie,
Of human kind the truest and the best,
For when her husband was about to die,
Unless his place she would herself supply,
For him she chose to die and go to hell,
And in his stead, among the dead to dwell."

Cassandra goes, and he with hardened heart
At anger of her speech forgot his woe,
And from his bed now suddenly doth start,
As one who had been sick, but well doth grow;
For nothing now he cares except to know
The truth of what he must henceforth endure,
And in the truth to find his death or cure.

FORTUNE, controller of the permutation
Of things entrusted to her will and sway,
Yet subject to great Jove's administration,
Now making kingdoms slip and slide away,
And all things follow their appointed day,
Began to pluck the feathers bright of Troy,
And left both Troy and Trojans bare of joy.

Great Hector drew near to his period's end,
Which all too soon for Troy must now arrive;
Forth from his body fate his soul would send,
And sought a means upon its way to drive
It hence, against which he in vain might strive;
For into battle on a day he went,
Which ended only when his life was spent.

Now every man, it seems to me but right,
Who follows arms, should heartily bewail
The death of such a perfect noble knight!
As with his sword he did a king assail,
Achilles, unseen, pierced him through the mail,
And through his body drove the fatal dart
That stopped the beating of his knightly heart.

For this knight's death, so brave and generous,
The grief the Trojans felt no tongue can tell,
And least of all the grief of Troilus,
Who next to him was honor's source and well;
Such dark despair on Troilus now fell,
So utterly all joys his heart forsook,
For no day of relief he now doth look.

Nevertheless for all his grim despair,
For all his fear his lady was untrue,
Yet still his mind and thought turned ever there,

And like all lovers, still he sought anew
To justify his lady, bright of hue,
And to excuse her, he would often say,
That Calchas was the cause of this delay.

He even planned, should time and place permit,
To go and see her in a pilgrim's guise,
But feared he could not so well counterfeit,
That he might risk the test of searching eyes,
Nor find excuse for what men might surmise,
If he among the Greeks were ever caught,
And so he must relinquish this vain thought.

To Cressida he often wrote anew,
For not the faintest chance he would neglect,
Beseeching her that since he still was true,
His love, long proved, she should not thus reject;
And Cressida, for pity, I suspect,
Wrote him, as I shall tell, a parting word,
Which was the last he ever from her heard:

"THOU son of Cupid, model of all that's good,
Thou sword of knighthood, valor's primal source,
Pray how may she who long herself hath stood
In torment, sorrow from thy heart divorce?
Behold me, sad and sick, with no recourse,
Since you with me nor I with you may deal,
But helpless grief within me to conceal.

"Your letters ample and your paper plaints
Have deeply moved my heart to sympathy;
The stains of tears that broke their long restraints,
These have I seen, but what you ask of me,
To come to Troy, just now that cannot be,
Yet why, since someone may this letter seize,
I cannot here explain to you with ease.

"Grievous to me, God knows, is your unrest,
And what the Gods have ordered and ordained,
It seems you take it not as for the best,
And all the thought you have in mind retained
Is but of present pleasure unrestrained;
But for all that, I say 'tis only fear
Of wicked tongues that makes me linger here.

"For I have heard things much to my surprise,
Concerning you and me, and how we stand,
Which call for cautious action and for wise;
And I have heard that you have merely planned
To hold me at your beck and your command;
But let that pass—I can but in you see
All truth, and gentleness and honesty.

"Yes, I will come! But times are out of joint,
And as things stand with me, what year or day
That this shall be, I cannot now appoint.
But still, whatever happens, let me pray
To have your goodwill and your friendship aye,
For truly while my living days endure,
My friendship to you I do here assure.

"And I must ask you that you do not take
It ill, if I so briefly to you write;
I dare not, where I am, distrust awake,
Nor ever had I skill well to endite.
Brief words may cover more than meets the sight.
The meaning counts, and not the letters' space.
So fare you well! God grant to you his grace!
                                        LA VOSTRE C."

This letter Troilus thought rather strange,
And read it with a sad and thoughtful sigh,
For therein saw he many signs of change,
Yet to himself continued to deny
That she her faith and name would stultify.
However much their ladies may them grieve,
That they are false, what lover can believe!

But ever must a time come at the last
When truth will out for every man to see;
For now the day approaches, sure and fast,
When Troilus must realize that she
Was not as constant as she ought to be,
And that the love and faith that seemed so sure,
Were not so true that they could long endure.

One day he stood in melancholy thought,
For now his doubts of her he could not down,
But still they came unchallenged and unsought,

When through the length of all the Trojan town,
As happened oft with trophies of renown,
Before Deiphebus for all to see
An armor cloak was born in victory.

This cloak, as Lollius explains to us,
Deiphebus had torn from Diomede
That day, and in the throng was Troilus,
Regarding it with keen attentive heed;
Its length, its breadth, the work on it, their meed
Of praise he gave to all, and taking hold
Of it, he saw what made his blood run cold.

For on the collar lay hid there within,
A brooch which he to Cressida had given
Ere she left Troy, and on her breast did pin,
In witness of his love with sorrow riven;
And she an equal faith to show had striven,
And pledged to keep it aye, but now he knew
That to her word and him she was untrue.

He hastened home and straight for Pandar sent,
Recounting to him all the sad details
About the fatal brooch and what it meant;
His lady's falsity he then bewails
Against which love nor honor aught avails,
For death alone can heal this wound so sore,
And peace unto his shattered heart restore.

"O CRESSIDA," he cried, "O lady bright,
Where is your faith, where is your promised word!
Where are the love and truth that you did plight!
All these on Diomede are now conferred!
Alas, by shame you should have been deterred
From this, for though you might have been untrue,
No need was there such hateful deed to do!

"What man shall ever trust in oaths again?
I never dreamed that thou couldst alter so,
O Cressida, unless it might be then,
If I the first inconstancy should show!
O that thy tender heart could deal such blow!
Alas, the hateful deed that thou hast done,
An evil eminence for thee hath won!

"Was there no other brooch that you might use
With which your new love you might usher in,
But only that endeared one you must choose,
Which on your faithless breast I once did pin?
What end could you expect thereby to win,
Except with needless cruelty to tell
That in your heart I now no longer dwell?

"For now I see you utterly have cast
Me from your thought, and yet I cannot find
It in my heart, in spite of all that's passed,
To drive you for a moment from my mind!
O what a fate unnatural and blind,
That I must love the best on all this earth
The one who holds me of the slightest worth!

"O God above, this favor I request,
That I may meet, and soon, this Diomede,
For gladly would I try with him a test
Of strength and see his life's heart bleed!
O God, who ever dost and shouldst take heed
To further virtue and to punish wrong,
Take thou thy vengeance on him swift and strong!

"Thou, Pandar, who didst often fret and chide,
Because my dreams seemed credible to me,
O, would that more on them I had relied,
For now you see your niece's falsity!
In sundry ways both joy and misery
The Gods reveal in sleep for our behoof,
And here my dreams provide for this a proof.

"But now of this what need I further speak?
From this time forth I shall in warlike fray
My death embrace, in fight with any Greek,
And none too soon for me shall come that day!
But Cressida, whom I shall love for aye,
With one last word, I will myself defend,
My love hath merited a better end."

ALL these things Pandar heard and none denied,
For now the end was far too evident;
With only silence therefore he replied,
Sorrow for Troilus doth speech prevent,

And shame for Cressida's ill management;
Still as a stone he stood, nor answer made,
By grief and shame all utterly dismayed.

But at the last he spoke as best he could,
"My brother dear, I fear your trouble lies
Beyond my aid, and I am through for good
With Cressida, and her I now despise.
What I have done for you in this emprise,
Regarding not my honor nor my rest,
I did it, Troilus, all for the best.

"If anything I did still pleases thee,
Then I am glad, and for this treason now,
God knows it is a heavy blow to me.
If anything could ease your heart, I vow
That I would serve you, if I knew but how,
And as for Cressida, the while I live,
Her perjury I never shall forgive."

THIS brought but slight relief to Troilus,
Whose final fortunes quickly now unfold.
Cressida loves the son of Tydeus,
And Troilus hath naught but comfort cold!
Such is the world! Wherever you behold,
The common state of man is one of woe,
And in the end, we all must take it so!

In daily battles, as the days go by,
Doth Troilus, the noblest Trojan knight,
With courage by despair exalted high,
Exhibit all his valor and his might;
Now doth his wrath upon the Greeks alight,
But most of all he looked for Diomede,
For hate of him doth other hates exceed.

And oftentimes these two opponents met,
With bloody strokes and with exchange of speech;
Spear against spear they often thus did whet,
Yet neither pierced so deeply as to reach
The other's life, so matched was each to each;
This neat exchange blind fortune would not send
That neither one the other's life should end.

And if my purpose here had been to write
The arms of Troilus, and not the man,
Then could I of his battles much endite;
But of his love I've told since I began,
And shall continue so, as best I can.
His deeds of arms, if you could of them hear,
Read Dares, where they all in full appear.

O GENTLE ladies all, so bright of hue,
Let me beseech, although it had to be
That I should write of one who was untrue,
Put not the blame for what she did on me,
For all the books tell her iniquity;
Penelope the true, if I but could,
I'd rather praise, or fair Alceste the good.

And O ye men, of you naught need be said,
Except that ladies men have oft betrayed!
Bad luck to them and curses on their head,
Who with feigned words and plots so subtly laid
On simple minds their evil tricks have played!
Beware of wiles, O ladies, and take heed,
What lesson in my story you may read.

GO, LITTLE book, my little tragedy!
God grant thy maker ere his ending day,
May write some tale of happy poetry!
But, little book, of any poet's lay
Envy of heart here shalt thou not display,
But kiss the steps where pass through ages spacious,
Vergil and Ovid, Homer, Lucan and Statius.

And since there is so great diversity
In English, and in the writing of our tongue,
I pray to God that no man miswrite thee,
Or get thy meter wrong and all unstrung;
But everywhere that thou art read or sung,
I trust all men will take thee as they should—
But now to come back where my story stood.

THE wrath of Troilus, as I have said,
The Grecian warriors had to pay for dear,
And hosts of Greeks his valiant hand struck dead;

Though in his time he was without a peer
Within the city, yet the fatal spear
Of bold Achilles, as the gods had willed,
At early last this Trojan hero killed.

And when his final earthly breath he drew,
His spirit from his body lightly went,
And to the eighth sphere's hollow concave flew,
Leaving in convex every element,
And then he saw, in glorious ascent,
The wandering stars, and heard the harmony
Of all the spheres in heavenly melody.

And down from thence he cast his spirit's eyes
Upon this spot of earth, that with the sea
Is bound, and now doth heartily despise
This wretched world, with all its vanity,
In contrast with the joy in full degree
Of heaven above; and at the very last
His gaze where he was slain, he downward cast.

Silently he laughed to see the grief and woe
Of those who weep within this earthly space,
Renouncing all men's works, who only know
Those earthly joys which time shall soon efface;
In peace content with heaven's lasting grace,
His way he went, in rest no tongue can tell,
Where Mercury appointed him to dwell.

Thus ended, lo, the love of Troilus,
Thus ended, lo, this model of mankind;
His royal rank led to such end, and thus
Ended his high nobility of mind,
For this false world, so mutable and blind.
'Twas thus his love for Cressida began,
And thus until he died its full course ran.

YE YOUTH, so happy at the dawn of life,
In whom love springs as native to your days,
Estrange you from the world and its vain strife,
And let your hearts their eyes to him upraise
Who made you in his image! Give him praise,
And think this world is but a passing show,
Fading like blooms that all too briefly blow.

And love ye him who on the cross did buy
Our souls from timeless death to live for aye,
Who died and rose and reigns in heaven high!
Your deepest love his love will ne'er betray,
Your faith on him I bid you safely lay;
And since his love is best beyond compare,
Love of the world deny with all its care.

HERE, lo, the vanity of pagan rites!
Lo, here, how little all their shrines avail!
Lo, here the end of worldly appetites!
Lo, here, how all the Gods at last shall fail,
Apollo, Jove and Mars and all the tale!
Lo, here the song that time hath held in fee,
Rescued from crumbling, grey antiquity!

O MORAL Gower, to thee this book I send,
And to thee, too, thou philosophical Strode,
And beg, if need be, ye will it amend,
And have my thank, for all such care bestowed.
To Christ, the crucified, whose blood hath flowed
For us, for mercy now I humbly pray,
And to the highest Lord these words I say:

O THOU Eternal Three and Two and One,
Reigning forever in One and Two and Three,
Boundless, but binding all through Father and Son,
From foes unseen and seen deliver me;
And blessed Jesus, turn our love to thee,
And through thy maiden Mother, meek and mild,
Let all our hearts to thee be reconciled!

DOVER · THRIFT · EDITIONS

POETRY

All books complete and unabridged. All 5³⁄₁₆" x 8¼", paperbound. Available at your book dealer, online at **www.doverpublications.com**, or by writing to Dept. GI, Dover Publications, Inc., 31 East 2nd Street, Mineola, NY 11501. For current price information or for free catalogs (please indicate field of interest), write to Dover Publications or log on to **www.doverpublications.com** and see every Dover book in print. Dover publishes more than 500 books each year on science, elementary and advanced mathematics, biology, music, art, literary history, social sciences, and other areas.